Rathcoole and th

T0166827

Maynooth Studies in Local History

SERIES EDITOR Raymond Gillespie

This volume is one of five short books published in the Maynooth Studies in Local History series in 2019. Like their predecessors they range widely over the local experience in the Irish past. Chronologically they focus on the late eighteenth and nineteenth centuries but they focus on problems that reappeared in almost every period of Irish history. They span the experience of rebellion in late eighteenth-century Dublin and the trauma of family relations and murder in the early nineteenth century. More mundane tasks such as the problem of managing the poor, the task of economic development through the shaping of infrastructure and the management of land also feature. Geographically they range across the length of the country from Dublin to Waterford by way of Carlow and westwards from Howth to Sligo. Socially they move from those living on the margins of society in Sligo through the urban middle classes of mid nineteenth-century Dublin to the prosperous world of the urban elite in Waterford. In doing so they reveal diverse and complicated societies that created the local past and present the range of possibilities open to anyone interested in studying that past. Those possibilities involve the dissection of the local experience in the complex and contested social worlds of which it is part as people strove to preserve and enhance their positions within their local societies. It also reveals the forces that made for cohesion in local communities and those that drove people apart, whether through large scale rebellion or through acts of inter-personal violence. Such studies of local worlds over such long periods are vital for the future since they not only stretch the historical imagination but provide a longer perspective on the development of society in Ireland and help us to understand more fully the complex evolution of the Irish experience. These works do not simply chronicle events relating to an area within administrative or geographically determined boundaries, but open the possibility of understanding how and why particular regions had their own personality in the past. Such an exercise is clearly one of the most exciting challenges for the future and demonstrates the vitality of the study of local history in Ireland.

Maynooth Studies in Local History: Number 143

Rathcoole and the United Irish Rebellions, 1798–1803

Kerron Ó Luain

FOUR COURTS PRESS

Set in 10pt on 12pt Bembo by
Carrigboy Typesetting Services for
FOUR COURTS PRESS LTD
7 Malpas Street, Dublin 8, Ireland
www.fourcourtspress.ie
and in North America for
FOUR COURTS PRESS
c/o IPG, 814 N Franklin St, Chicago, IL 60610

ISBN 978–1–84682–804–1

Printed in Ireland
by SprintPrint, Dublin.

Contents

Acknowledgments

Many thanks are due to Dr Niall Ó Cíosáin for his advice during the course of my research for the MA dissertation from which this work originates. Also to Dr Caitríona Clear, co-ordinator of the MA course in Galway at the time of my research, and to my colleagues who undertook the same course for their conviviality. I also wish to express my gratitude to the staff at the National Library, National Archives, Trinity College Library, Dublin, the James Hardiman Library, National University of Ireland, Galway, and Tallaght Library, Dublin, who provided kind assistance as always. I am indebted to Professor Raymond Gillespie for providing me with the opportunity to publish my research in the Maynooth Studies in Local History series. Thanks are also due to Brian Casey who read a draft of the work and offered suggestions and to Caoimhín Ó Cadhla who advised me on a particular aspect of the 1790s. Finally, I wish to thank my family for their consistent support and I would also like to pay tribute to those friends, and others, with whom I spent my time in Galway a decade ago; many of them are gone now, but are not forgotten. Go raibh maith agaibh uilig.

Introduction

Passing in a south-westerly direction through present day Rathcoole, Co. Dublin, two remnants of the 18th century appear almost immediately upon entering the village. Rathcoole House, home to the young United Irish recruit John Clinch, and the Church of Ireland church stand only yards from one another. For many years passers-by would have been unaware of Rathcoole's deep connection with the 1798 rebellion. Unlike in Co. Wexford, where statues of pikemen stand proudly in town centres, Rathcoole displayed no such markers until the bicentenary commemorative events of the rising took place in 1998. That year, a plinth was constructed near the Court of Petty Sessions in the centre of the village, while a small plaque was erected on the Church of Ireland church wall. The plinth commemorates those from the locality associated with the rising and the plaque remembers two local bakers shot dead by crown forces. These two markers are the only existing suggestion that the area may have experienced a major rebellious convulsion in years gone by. To the modern observer, Rathcoole and its environs are of little historical significance. A more visible and detailed marker, which would explain in greater depth the experience of 1798 in the locality, is long overdue.

In the late 1790s and the early part of the 19th century, Rathcoole and its inhabitants bore witness to a series of chaotic, localized events. These events had their origins in national, and even international, political forces – forces that set in train monumental shifts in Irish society. Historians such as Tommy Graham have sought to place the disaffection and rebellion of the 1790s and early 19th century in the context of politics and politicization, thus moving away from agrarian and sectarian explanations.[1] Likewise, Jim Smyth has characterized arguments that portray the rising as a peasant *Jaquerie* as 'inadequate and patronizing', pointing to the 'complex stratification of rural society and the political dimension of the insurrection'. For Smyth, the charge of the rising as a sectarian affair, though more difficult to dismiss, by focussing on massacres such as Scullabogue, is reductionist and ignores the exceptionally politicized nature of counties such as Wexford.[2] Kevin Whelan has similarly sought to contextualize the rising in Wexford within the framework of politicization and polarization in the county from the 1760s.[3] Moving into the post-1798 years, James Patterson has also qualified what he calls the 'sectarian interpretation' where the historiography has pushed a narrative that the rising led to a total polarizing rift between Catholic and Protestant and republicanism was submerged under a sea of religious animosity.[4]

This study, by examining the emergence of radicalism among Rathcoole's locals, seeks to reinforce the political interpretation of the 1798 and 1803 rebellions on a national scale. It aims to discern the ideologies and social structures that propelled Rathcoole's locals into playing a part in shaping history and to consider what, if anything, may have rendered the locality peculiar and what may have allowed it fit into the wider pattern of politicization and unrest experienced elsewhere in Ireland. The phenomenon of polarization between opposing political, religious and social groups, and the limits of such a process, will also be discussed within the particular local context, as will the often personal and class-based nature of such tensions. As Gillespie and Moran have written, a better understanding of how different social networks, or 'communities of interest', in different regions adopted or rejected various political ideas contributes to comprehending the growth of Irish nationalism on a countrywide level.[5] This work aims to add to that endeavour by assessing some of the communities of interest in Rathcoole during the 1790s. The first chapter will set the social context for the rising by documenting the land structures and class divisions in Rathcoole while noting the village's religious composition, issues of great importance in shaping events elsewhere. It shall then trace the emergence of radical politics in Rathcoole and the key local figures who were central to that development. The second chapter shall focus on the course of the rising in Rathcoole and its vicinity. Why was the rising foiled in Rathcoole and what was the village's relationship, in military terms, with both Dublin city and the wider north Leinster region? The chapter shall also attempt to assess the character of events during the summer of 1798. Was sectarianism a factor in the violence? Did the rebels harbour class-based enmities or personal grudges? As local studies are not solely about static administrative boundaries and the events that occurred within them, but are really about people and communities, this chapter will also trace the activities of local man Felix Rourke in his activities in Meath and Kildare during 1798. Finally, in the third chapter, the existence of post-rebellion disaffection and a continuity in republicanism as a precursor to a second rising in 1803 shall be documented, as will the efforts of local powerbrokers to contain and manage such disaffection.

A variety of primary source material was utilized in this regard. Some of the material such as the Rebellion Papers, stored in the National Archives, which emanated from local powerbrokers, was top-down in nature. In terms of Rathcoole, the papers deal largely with magistrates' and informants' accounts of rebel activity in the area and are confined primarily to the years 1798–1803 when United Irish organization spiked and government attention was most focussed. As Deirdre Lindsay has commented with regard to the Rebellion Papers, correspondence from liberal quarters is rare. 'The bulk of this material consists of private letters written to Dublin Castle, for the most part by those who would have described themselves as "friends of government" – people such as resident gentry, clergymen, local government office-holders, magistrates'.[6] Even so, there is some correspondence in the Rebellion Papers to balance that of the hostile administration. This was written in the main by those Rathcoole inhabitants who were sympathetic towards the rebels and corresponded with government seeking their release in the wake of the insurrection. The State Prisoners' Petitions, also housed in the National Archives, likewise balance unsympathetic government accounts and illustrate the outlook of the liberal minor gentry in Rathcoole who sought lenience for imprisoned local rebels. The State Prisones' Petitions provide insight into which side of the contemporary political spectrum some of Rathcoole's local propertied class were located. James Ormsby's map held in the National Library was an important source in documenting the property holdings of this class and also displayed the survival of commonage in the area in the 1790s – both important in assessing the locality's social structure.

In contrast to other parishes, no records such as vestry minute books are held in the Representative Church Body library for the Church of Ireland in Rathcoole. Such sources can provide a window into the social structure of a particular area, as tithe payments and a register of landowners were logged in them, among other documentation such as minute books for community organizations that might have given a deeper understanding of the wealthier sections of Rathcoole society. The records of baptisms, marriages and burials for Rathcoole between the years 1724 and 1889 have also unfortunately disappeared. Both of these sources for the area were likely lost during the Free State attack on the Four Courts which destroyed the Public Record Office during the Civil War in 1922.

Nevertheless, the letters of the Clancy household of Ballymount represent an invaluable resource that sheds light on the political outlook of that propertied class and the social structure which worked to its advantage. The letters of the Church of Ireland family begin in 1797 and continue with some frequency through the following year of rebellion.[7] They demonstrate the effect the rebellion had in polarizing the locality into groups in favour of insurgency and radical political change – and therefore often against the propertied class – versus those who defended the status quo. The letters also document the personal and intimate aspect of the rebellion where servants and farm labourers turned against their wealthier strong farmer or gentry masters. The fear with which the propertied class viewed the lower orders is also palpable in the Clancy letters.[8]

The letters, furthermore, contain one of the few references to women having taken part in the rebellion in their area. Indeed, most of the official correspondence and press reportage of the insurgents fails to note composition. As Bartlett has pointed out, despite having fulfilled roles as activists and combatants, women were neglected in the historiography of the rebellion for many years due to the social mores of the 19th and 20th centuries. During the rising and in its aftermath, no woman was treated as a state prisoner or court martialled, largely due to the mistaken perception that the rebellion was entirely the work of men.[9] Such views quite likely influenced the character of the source material available for Rathcoole where women were also marginalized.

Many of the reports of rebel activity were found in Dublin-based newspapers such as the *Freeman's Journal*, with a number of organs printed in London also of some use. However, these reports were frequently characterized by propaganda, exaggeration and mistruths. They can, nevertheless, be utilized when placed in their appropriate context or balanced by other accounts. To this end Robert Madden's *The United Irishmen; their lives and times* was invaluable. As C.J. Woods has noted of Madden's magnum opus, the tone was favourable towards the republican cause. 'He sought to rehabilitate the United Irishmen, to lend them respectability and to explain their rebellion as an inevitable consequence of bad government'.[10] Importantly, the second volume of Madden's four-volume undertaking contains a memoir of Rathcoole's primary protagonist during the rebellion years, Felix Rourke. The memoir is actually taken from accounts given to Madden by Rourke's close friends and associates. Its content is matter of fact in most places except where Rourke's own letters are included. Rourke's letters were all written while he was confined in Naas gaol following the rebellion. Although the letters do not extend to the pre-rebellion period and answer the questions of how, and why, Rourke and many of Rathcoole's inhabitants moved towards radical politics during the 1790s, they offer valuable insight into the attitudes of Rathcoole's most prominent United Irishman and make clear his thoughts on a number of events of major importance that were occurring outside the walls of his cell.

The most important source in tracing the strategy of Rathcoole's United Irish rebels during the rebellion itself, and government plans to counteract it, was Richard Musgrave's *Memoirs of the different rebellions in Ireland*. Musgrave, a member of the Protestant gentry from Co. Waterford, was one of the chief chroniclers of the rebellion and the first edition of his account was published in 1802. In contrast to Madden, Musgrave's work was overtly sectarian in nature and, according to Patrick Comerford, he 'laboured the assertion that the real aim of the revolt was to exterminate Protestants'.[11] James Kelly, meanwhile, has placed emphasis on Musgrave's legacy as having fixed 'the attitude of a generation of British and Irish Protestants in stern opposition to Catholic emancipation'.[12] Musgrave's handiwork must therefore be treated critically, despite its value in tracing local rebel movements.

What long-term developments produced figures such as Musgrave, the Protestant Ascendancy of which he was a member, and a majority Catholic population which was disenfranchised? The defeat of the Gaelic chieftains by the English at the battle of Kinsale in 1601 during the Nine Years War and their subsequent flight six years later in 1607 – known as the 'Flight of the earls' – opened up the way for an expansion of England's colonial conquest of Ireland.[13]

Systematic plantations of Protestant settlers into parts of Ireland, intended to suppress the rebellious native population, had been underway since the 16th century. With the fall of the Gaelic Ulster chieftains, plantations began to be undertaken in the early 17th century in the north, until that point the remaining stronghold of resistance to the English. These were followed by the Cromwellian land confiscations of the mid-17th century, which transferred vast swathes of the country to Protestant ownership, dispossessing Catholics in the process. The minority Protestant Ascendancy, which held sway following these land grabs, defended its position with gusto. The defeat of James II's claim at the battle of the Boyne by William of Orange in 1690 pushed Catholic Ireland into further hardship. Following the defeat, Penal Laws, which limited the rights of both Catholics *and* Presbyterians in a range of spheres from landholding to employment, were introduced to protect the special position of the Anglican elite.[14]

As the threat of politico-religious war subsided, and what remained of the Catholic aristocracy consistently declared loyalty throughout the 18th century, some of these laws began to be abolished. Inspired by the American Revolution of 1776, a colonial form of nationalism developed among many Irish Protestants. This body of opinion was encapsulated by the Volunteer movement, which demanded an independent Irish legislature from the British government. Cautious of being dealt a similar blow to that dealt by the Americans, the British government relented and 'Grattan's parliament' – so-called after the movement's figurehead Henry Grattan – was established in 1782. In reality, the parliament on College Green in Dublin was based on a system of patronage, and excluded the vast bulk of the population. Through the British government appointed lord lieutenant, Ireland was still effectively under Westminster control. As the century progressed, upper- and middle-class Catholics, for their part, continued to seek political reform, the right to vote and access to public office. With the onset of war between Britain and France from 1778 more of the Penal Laws were scrapped. Further Catholic relief was conceded in the early 1790s when British aristocratic fears were stoked by the French Revolution of 1789. However, inspired by the French example and by the principles of liberty, equality and fraternity that it seemed to embody, Irish radicals, many of them Protestant Dissenters, founded the Society of United Irishmen in 1791. The United Irishmen sought to push for more political reform than the British government, and its largely Anglican allies in Ireland, was willing to concede. As a result, the republican United Irishmen gradually moved to a revolutionary separatist position.[15] This inherent conflict reached breaking point at both the local and national level during the 1790s, culminating in the 1798 rebellion.

1. Local society and the emergence of radical politics

Rathcoole lies nearly 10 miles south-west of Dublin city. It is nestled in the extremities of the Dublin hills with the Wicklow mountains lying further to the south and the plains of mid-Leinster beginning on the village's western periphery (fig. 1). The defining geographical feature of Rathcoole during the 18th century was the main road which cut through the centre of the village and ran from Dublin to Kilcullen via Naas, and southwards to Munster. Rathcoole was the first village on the road out of Dublin and was frequently used as a stop-over for traffic travelling south. Another road branched off this primary route at the west end of the village and led on to Ballymore-Eustace, Co. Kildare.[1] The road between Dublin and Kilcullen was the first portion of the Munster toll road. After 1789, the operation of the post office mail service stimulated villages on the new mail coach roads as they received trade and quarterly tolls from the passing postal coaches.[2] Rathcoole was therefore an important communications and military strategic point and a garrison was maintained in the village to provide an armed presence.

In 1837, Samuel Lewis, a popular publisher of topographical dictionaries, wrote that the parish of Rathcoole comprised 4,005 statute acres, and that its lands were fertile 'and generally under profitable cultivation'.[3] According to *Griffith's valuation* – undertaken from 1848 – the land with the highest net value lay to the north of the village at Collegelands where the enclosures were also largest. In and around the village smaller parcels of land with moderate net values were typical, while the mountainous reaches to the south in the townlands of Slademore, Slievethoul and Redgap contained land of lower values.[4]

In the 18th century observers who passed through Rathcoole by road remarked upon the impoverished state of the village's inhabitants. In 1732, John Loveday, a famed contemporary traveller, noted that the road was well constructed and exceptionally wide, but he described the people of the area as having been inflicted with great poverty. He encountered shabby mud cabins, which he was surprised to see in such close proximity to the capital.[5] There had been little change in this regard when 40 years later another traveller, Thomas Campbell, commented in his *Philosophical survey* as he journeyed through Rathcoole in 1775, that the village was 'mostly composed of clay huts, which are sometimes, you know, both warm and neat; but these were so awkwardly built, and so irregularly arranged, that even Wales would have been ashamed of them'.[6] Philip Luckombe echoed these exact sentiments four years later when

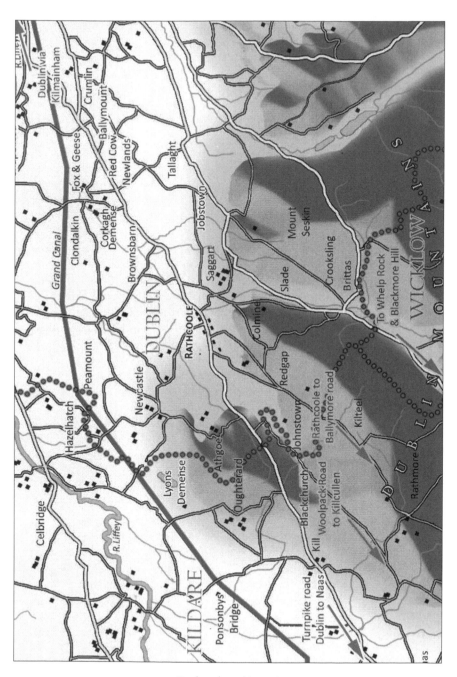

1. Rathcoole and its region

in 1779 he passed through the village on his tour of Ireland.[7] Support for the evidence of the travellers who came across poverty and shoddy cabins as they passed through Rathcoole is indicated by a *Freeman's Journal* report of January 1791 which described a roadside cabin near the village as having been blown down by the wind, leading to the death of a man and woman who were inside at the time.[8] As R.A. Butlin, in his study of agriculture in late-18th-century Co. Dublin, has maintained; 'the most striking contrast [lay] between the affluence of 18th-century Dublin society, both county and city ... and the extreme poverty of the landless and near landless cottars and labourers'.[9]

This situation of vast inequality persisted into the early 19th century when Joseph Archer wrote in 1801, in his *Statistical survey of the county of Dublin*, that many of the cottiers of the county were 'wretchedly provided with habitation'. He noted that thatch was more widespread than slate or tiles and he remarked that these 'hovels' were prone to burning and infestation by vermin. The cottier and labourer class clothed themselves in a cheap, strong and warm material known as frieze, which they purchased at local fairs. The mainstay food of the cottiers was potatoes and milk. If potatoes became too expensive they were substituted by bread or a mix of oatmeal and water known as 'stirabout'. In the more remote parts of the county farmers accommodated cottiers and labourers in return for work or a small rent. Obtaining fuel was a problem and hedges were cut down wantonly, although those who lived in or near mountainous areas had access to turf.[10] Turf, known elsewhere as peat, was cut from bog lands and used for cooking and heating and was vital for the survival of many families.

Although life was tough for many of Rathcoole's locals, pastimes such as horseracing acted as a welcome distraction, with races reported as having been held in the village in 1782,[11] while in nearby Clondalkin a 'steeple chase' took place in 1793.[12] As James Kelly has noted, there were horse-racing courses in both Rathcoole and Clondalkin during the second half of the 18th century. The gentry offered patronage to many of the race meetings, which were major social occasions. Drinking tents were erected and gambling and fox hunts took place to coincide with the meetings, some of which lasted for up to a week.[13]

Rathcoole's population was predominantly Catholic. John D'Alton, in his *The history of the county of Dublin*, noted that in 1831 the Anglican parish of Newcastle, of which Rathcoole was a part, comprised of '1,489 persons, of whom it is stated that not forty were Protestants'.[14] The first government statistics that documented the area's confessional balance, available in the 1861 census, reflect a similarly overwhelming Catholic majority as that recorded thirty years earlier by D'Alton. Out of a total population of 1,139 in 1861, Rathcoole's rural district and village combined was home to 1,063 Catholics but only 72 members of the Church of Ireland and four Presbyterians. Catholics, therefore, accounted for 93 per cent of the population. Nearby Saggart and Newcastle and their rural hinterlands displayed similar Catholic majorities.[15] Even allowing for demographic shifts over several decades it seems clear that Catholics made up the vast bulk of the populace in Rathcoole during the 1790s.

According to contemporary observers, the language change that had been underway for some time, which saw English replace Irish as the vernacular, had already allegedly occurred for the most part in Co. Dublin by the late 18th century. Writing in 1801, Archer stated that 'the English language is the general one spoken in this county; very few are in the habit of speaking Irish, nor do many understand it, except those that have removed here from remoter counties'.[16] However, Nicholas Wolf's recent pioneering study on the language has demonstrated how Irish persisted in a dynamic way in the century up to 1870 and was employed by speakers in a range of interactions with church, state and nationalist politicians.[17] Ó Cadhla, meanwhile, has documented the existence of numerous Irish-language songs written about the rebellion in its aftermath.[18] Such evidence casts doubt on the observations of foreign travellers such as Archer regarding the demise of the language during the 1790s. Besides, the era of mass literacy in English would not dawn until after the establishment of the National Schools in 1831.[19]

During the 18th century, only one educational institution which encouraged literacy was founded in Rathcoole when a charter school was established in the village in 1744. Mary Mercer's school, built as an alms house for poor girls in the area, stood at the west end of the village. Mercer was a spinster who had come into money. She wished to donate her wealth to charitable causes and she also assisted in the founding of Mercer's hospital in the city. The school opened its doors in April 1745 with some 20 girls enrolled. The entire cost of construction was £742 6s. 4½d. with the sum of £100 being made available for furniture and equipment. Indicating the class and business interests of the school's trustees, they had also considered letting the inn in Rathcoole, which was known by a sign with a white horse and a black lion. The inn was on 14 acres of land and had recently belonged to Matthew Bermingham and David Birtchell. Catholic parents who had initially opted to send their children to the charter school soon became suspicious that their children were being exposed to the Protestant faith and withdrew them from the school. By 1750 the trustees had decided to permit only those pupils whose father and mother could be proven to be Protestants to attend. The denominational nature of the school meant that its impact in spreading literacy in the area was limited. An inscription on the gates of the school had left no doubt as to the institution's aims. It read: 'For the education of poor girls in the Protestant religion by the bequest of Mary Mercer, spinster, this hospital was erected and endowed 1744'.[20] The school was a prominent social landmark in the village and survived the years of rebellion despite its exclusivist nature. The rebels certainly managed to come within a couple of hundred yards of the school building as the nearby property of John Mullan was razed during 1798.[21] The surviving records show no major impact on the school during the rebellion, a fact that indicates that sectarian tensions in the area were not as pronounced as in other places, such as Castlecarbery, Co. Kildare, where, during 1798, as many as 2,000 rebels attacked and burned the Protestant charter school which had been previously abandoned by Stephen Sparks and his students.[22]

By the 1820s formal schooling in the area had still not developed in any significant way. In 1821 the Catholic parish of Saggart, of which Rathcoole was a part, recorded a population of 1,400. Yet the census of that year noted that only 33 of those (20 boys and 13 girls) attended school under the patronage of the Trinitarian Orphan Society.[23] An inquiry into Irish education conducted by the government in 1826 listed the same school as a Catholic establishment that charged some pupils a fee and allowed others attend for free. Although the attendance at the school had risen to 97, the building was described as 'a thatched house, in very bad repair'. The school continued under the patronage of the Trinitarians and paid Francis Brady for each child taught, his income amounting to £35 annually.[24] Despite the school having been funded by the Trinitarians, a Catholic order, it is likely a large proportion of the parish's Catholic inhabitants were still illiterate in the 1820s. Projecting backwards with suitable caution, illiteracy was, therefore, more prevalent among the Catholic population in the parish during the 1790s when no such Catholic school existed. Ó Gráda has remarked that hedge schools, usually run by a single teacher and demanding a fee from the students, provided a degree of literacy in the decades prior to the founding of the National Schools in 1831. He has estimated that as far back as the 1760s about 40 per cent of the country's males could read and write with less than half being totally illiterate.[25] Due to the restricted nature of Mercer's Protestant only girls' school during the 18th century and the ineffectual state of Catholic religious schooling in the area later on in the 1820s, the only estimation of literacy in English in Rathcoole during the 1790s must be based on Ó Gráda's national figures deduced from hedge school attendance: 40 per cent of males literate (able to read and write) with over 50 per cent able to read.

Although Mercer's charter schoolhouse represented a symbol of the state religion in Rathcoole during the 1790s it was, as in other towns and villages, the Church of Ireland building (fig. 2) that embodied the preferential treatment afforded to the Established Church in the area. Rathcoole's Church of Ireland church, consecrated in 1738, commanded a high position above the main road through the village, with the graveyard of the area's ascendancy also visible to passers-by. The Church of Ireland parish of Rathcoole included the townland of Calliaghstown to the west and was linked with the parish of Newcastle-Lyons. The vicarage was the property of the archbishop, while the tithes were paid to the dean and chapter of St Patrick's Cathedral.[26] The tithes collected from the church were valued at £310 annually, with the vicar entitled to retain £60 of that amount.[27]

Despite the vestry book having been lost, one surviving entry from its pages exists in another source, A short history of Rathcoole, published in 1898. The entry

2. Rathcoole church

from the vestry book mentions economy lands enclosed by the church in 1737 and the collection of £32. 16s. 5d. in rent in the form of both cash and arrears. The lands in question were leased to John Ponder for £50 for an unknown period. The money raised was used for the re-construction of the church. It appears that the lease was then renewed by act of Vestry in 1748 to Richard Green for a term of thirty years, to commence in 1778. The rent or the exact land he leased is not known but there was a stipulation included in the lease that he repair the churchyard wall and erect a new gate.[28] At the time of the 1798 rebellion, Joseph Elwood, a Derryman, was the vicar of Rathcoole church. Elwood held the position between 1771 and 1804. He had been educated in Trinity College, Dublin, before returning to perform the duties of curator in his home county. Elwood then returned to Dublin to act as curator of St Catherine's Church on Thomas Street before obtaining the post of vicar at Rathcoole, which he held until his resignation from church duties in 1804.[29]

As was the case throughout the country tithes and their collection would have fostered resentment among Rathcoole's peasantry. The Whiteboy secret societies of 1760s Munster had reacted violently against tithes. However, as Michael Beames has pointed out, their motives were not always political or religious and Catholic clergy were also liable to be attacked when charges for mass, confession and other church practices were deemed excessive.[30] Nevertheless, the notion of those who resided in mud cabins in Rathcoole having been forced to offer up a tenth of their produce to a church that was alien to them and to a figure from outside the area such as Elwood, as well as some locals having probably worked the lands around the church for Mr Ponder and Mr Green, is sufficient to suggest that some degree of antipathy existed in the locality towards the Established Church.

The Penal Laws had left the locality's Catholics in a far less organized state in terms of their religious institutions and they only came to assert themselves gradually as the 18th century progressed. In the early part of the century, according to the *Report on the state of popery in Ireland 1731*, Catholics had no church or priest in Rathcoole. Nearby Newcastle was better organized, being home to one 'mass-house' and one 'popish school' with at least two priests listed as residing there. Several other priests were also suspected of living in the parish by a hostile administration, who attempted to enumerate clergy who quite likely did not want to be enumerated.[31] By 1794, at least, the parish of Saggart, which included Rathcoole, had been allocated its own Catholic cleric, Fr Harold, whom we shall encounter again in later chapters.

Rathcoole's economy and class structure were not dissimilar to that of other small villages on Dublin's periphery. The aforementioned travellers of leisure such as Loveday, Campbell and Luckombe, and indeed those going about more routine business and passing through the village to the south towards Munster and north towards Dublin, provided a source of income for the propertied class of Rathcoole. The Munster King Inn Hotel was a sizeable establishment in the middle of the village, which acted as a changing station on the coach road. The seven acres of land on which the inn stood was church land and was leased to John Ponder in 1736. By 1788 the inn had passed into the hands of Thomas Ransford as the following advertisement carried in the *Dublin Evening Post* of 5 January that year makes clear:

GREAT INN IN RATHCOOLE

Thomas Ransford – Returns his sincere thanks to the Nobility and Public for their great encouragement since his commencement in business, begs leave to inform them that he has at great expense fitted up his house in the neatest manner with good wines, &c. and from his great care and attention to his business hopes for the protection of his Friends and the Public as long as he shall be found deserving of it. *N.B.* – He has excellent Post Carriages and Horses ready at Rathcoole and in Dublin, by applying at John Nevil's No. 19 Duke Street or at Patt. McCan's, No. 1 Princes Street.[32]

Other members of the village's middle class such as a Mr Leedom, who kept 'an inn of great quality' in Rathcoole around 1789, also benefited from the village's position on the high road. The lower classes, however, had only limited employment options. Although there was a large paper mill in nearby Saggart that provided work for some locals, no major industrial growth ever took place in Rathcoole and by the 1830s the village retained the label of being primarily a 'post town' on the main road.[33] Indeed, Archer had earlier noted in 1801 that Co. Dublin's paper mills had gone into a general decline. The manufacturers, he wrote, 'say they have not sufficient rags, and that there is not a smart demand for what they do make'.[34] As Seán Bagnall has noted, the nearby parish of Tallaght saw no real commercial growth throughout most of the 19th century in spite of its proximity to Dublin. The availability of shops and markets in the capital hindered the development of those facilities in Tallaght and the possibility of a strong shop-keeping lower middle class emerging.[35]

In the late 18th century, most of Rathcoole's inhabitants and those in the surrounding countryside lived off their association with the land. Indeed, over two decades later the census of 1821 documented how 248 out of the 363 persons enumerated as having been employed in Saggart parish were 'persons chiefly employed in agriculture'. This amounted to over two-thirds, or 68 per cent, having been engaged in working the land. Only 44 persons, or roughly 12 per cent, of those listed as having had occupations were employed in trades, manufacture or handicrafts, while 77, or 21 per cent, were employed in other occupations. The nearby parish of Newcastle revealed a similar figure for those engaged in agriculture of 58 per cent.[36] Even considering the decline of domestic industry such as spinning in the face of steam powered industrialization and British competition during the 19th century,[37] it is clear that the vast majority of Rathcoole's inhabitants were dependent on the land for their income during the 1790s. According to Butlin, during the course of the 1700s the capital's increasing influence and rising population placed demands on places such as Rathcoole for agricultural produce, establishing a symbiosis with the city.[38] Economically, Rathcoole and its immediate hinterland stood firmly in the shadow of Dublin.

Landowning structures in Rathcoole and in many areas in the south of Co. Dublin during the late 18th century differed from those of the vast estates on the plains of Meath and Kildare to the west. The majority of land in and around Rathcoole belonged to the Protestant archbishop of Dublin, which enabled remnants of influence from the Pale's feudal times to endure.[39] One such example was the continued existence of narrow 'strip' holdings associated with common and open fields which harked back to agrarian arrangements of old. This method of farming was known as rundale and similar patterns prevailed in nearby Saggart and Clondalkin. Ormsby's map of Rathcoole drawn (fig. 3) in 1792 shows large-scale agrarian organization, with 18 proprietors sharing 312 acres and 14 perches of arable, meadow and croft land. Each holding was minutely sub-divided and scattered throughout the fields.[40] Mr Buckley, who we shall encounter again later, was the largest proprietor holding some 61 acres divided into 66 parcels of land.[41] This common land covered up to 600 acres and stretched into the foothills of the Dublin and Wicklow mountains. It was

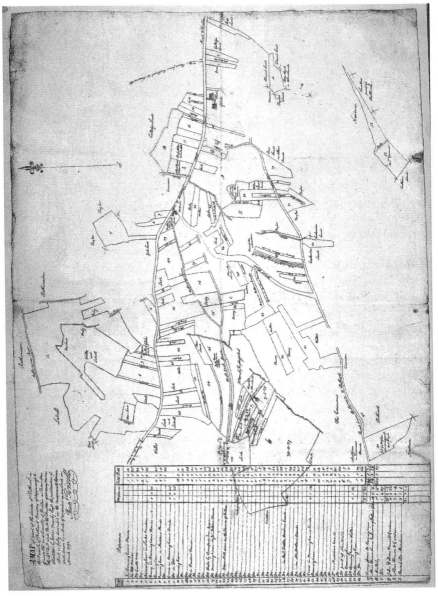

3. Ormsby's map of Rathcoole, 1792

not enclosed until 1818. In 1837 Lewis noted that 'Rathcoole has a patent for holding fairs on April 23rd, June 18th and October 9th, but these fairs have not been held for some years'.[42] The fairs took place on the commons and were held during the 1790s, with the enclosure of the land in 1818 having put an end to them.[43]

There was a notable absence of major landed gentry figures in Rathcoole during the 18th century. Kevin Whelan, in his work on neighbouring Newcastle, about two miles to the north-west of Rathcoole, has concluded that the lack of backing from a single landlord led to a period of stagnation in the village.[44] The Lawless family acquired the Lyons estate towards the close of the 18th century. The demesne skirted the Dublin/Kildare border close to Celbridge and was home to Nicholas Lawless, the first Lord Cloncurry, one of the wealthiest men in the country. His heir, Valentine Brown Lawless, who, as recently documented by Karina Holton, later became an influential liberal politician during the 19th century, counted United Irishmen such as Lord Edward FitzGerald, the Emmet brothers, Hamilton Rowan and Wolfe Tone among his friends.[45] But, according to Whelan, Newcastle was 'split between a number of small landowners, none of whom had the "clout" to turn it into a properly functioning estate village', and by the time the Lawless family had taken up residence the chance of establishing a prosperous estate village had passed.[46]

Newcastle was also the nearest seat of parliamentary power to Rathcoole. A pocket borough, it had twelve burgesses who were for the most part absentees. It was alleged by one source that those who held the franchise in the borough were numerous as it was 'well inhabited by persons of independent properties'.[47] Toward the close of the 18th century, Newcastle was described as a dilapidated village and attention was given to the fact that it returned the same number of MPs as the City of Dublin and Trinity College. The borough was controlled by the Latouches, a powerful landowning family in Kildare who owned most the lands around Newcastle. Both John and David Latouche were returned to serve in the house of commons in 1783.[48] The family's dominance of the constituency was illustrated by the fact that the last election held in the borough in 1797, before its disenfranchisement by the act of Union in 1800, returned David Latouche and a new generation of the family, his son and namesake David Latouche Jr.[49]

Rathcoole suffered similar neglect in political representation to that of Newcastle during the first half of the 18th century during which time its chief resident was a Mr Clement Barry, and the sources only referred to the village's position on the road southwards. The latter half of the century saw Edward Kennedy settle in Johnstown just outside the village. At the time of the 1798 rebellion Kennedy held the position of local magistrate.[50] It was not until his son, John Kennedy, began to purchase land around Rathcoole in 1813, and was made a baronet in 1836, that the area had a resident of some political stature.[51] A year later in 1837 Lewis noted that the main seat of power in Rathcoole was in Johnstown where John Kennedy owned a 'tastefully disposed and well cultivated demesne of 200 acres'.[52] To compound matters, the only individual to hold a peerage (a lifetime title) associated with Rathcoole was an absentee figure. Lord Viscount of Rathcoole, Charles Tracy, was presented with a burgess of the shire (a type of title bestowed on MPs in borough constituencies) in 1773.[53] Later, in 1789, Tracy received the king's authority to take the surname and arms of Leigh.[54] A member of the house of lords, it appears that Tracy took no interest in the Rathcoole locality and had no input into the development of the area. *The gentleman's and citizen's almanack* of 1786 listed his town residence as London and his country residence as Gloucestershire.[55] Tracy was not mentioned in any contemporary sources relating to Rathcoole, nor did he own any tracts of land in the area or act as a local figure of authority. The most prominent political figure to reside in the vicinity of Rathcoole was Lord Kilwarden who lived three miles away at Newlands. He was returned as an MP to the Irish house of commons from 1783 to 1790 for Coleraine and throughout the whole of the 1790s for the boroughs of James' and the city of Dublin as well as for Ardfert, Co. Kerry. He also held a number of prominent positions in the legal system as well as receiving a peerage in 1800.[56] Despite his prominence in city life and national politics his influence does not seem to have extended to Rathcoole as he owned no lands there and consequently appears to have had no dealings with the village or its inhabitants. It is clear then that 'the age of improvement' by-passed Rathcoole before any figure with the means, the standing, or the ambition, emerged to fund its development. As a result, an estate village with landlord-backed industries, churches and schools never materialized in the area.

The primary landowners in the Rathcoole area, many of them also absentees, were Bermingham, Locke, Ormsby, Proby, Dillon, Bees and Waller. The Luttrells, who were as prominent as they were despised in the Clonsilla area of west Dublin, also owned land at Rathcoole, but exercised their influence chiefly at Luttrellstown Castle and demesne 10 miles to the north.[57] The aforementioned minor-gentry figures owned or leased most of the land around the centre of the village and on its western periphery, while the lands to the east in the direction of Saggart belonged almost entirely to the Established Church and the archbishop of Dublin.[58] The Waller family also owned a number of scattered tracts of land in Rathcoole, but they did not reside permanently in the area during this period. Sir Robert Waller lived in the city and died in 1783. His son sold a portion of the lands he inherited to James Ormsby in 1789. The Ormsbys also owned a residence in Dawson Street in Dublin, giving an indication of that family's wealth.[59] Waller, who lived well outside the area in Tipperary, retained possession of a number of acres, some of which he shared with Luttrell.[60] To the north-west of the village at Athgoe the Lockes were the main landowning family. The Lockes were an old Catholic gentry family who had survived the confiscations of the 17th century. A large Georgian house was built at Athgoe Park by John Locke in the first half of the 18th century. His grandson Peter Warren Locke was the last of his line to live at Athgoe, residing there during the turbulent years of the rising.[61] John Locke, who found himself in financial difficulties during the mid-1780s,[62] also owned a residence not far from the Customs House in the city. Peter Locke appears to have held some sway locally during the 1790s unlike the absentee landowners connected to the area.[63]

As Liam Chambers has shown in his work *Rebellion in Kildare, 1790–1803*, the presence of prominent figures such as Lord Edward FitzGerald, who owned vast estates, precipitated politicization in the countryside around them throughout the 1790s.[64] Historian Thomas Pakenham has also described Kildare in similar terms as a county of 'great wooded demesnes and liberal landlords'.[65] In Wexford, wealthy Catholic families such as the Hays and Sweetmans used their local status to spread radical ideas among the populace. The involvement of Edward Hay in agitation on the Catholic question during the 1790s saw him emerge as an anti-government figure who, through his contacts with Dublin and France, cultivated revolutionary sentiment in Wexford.[66] The absence of similar major landlords or Catholic mercantile figures long involved in agitation for reform seems to have delayed the spread of radicalism in Rathcoole until the closing years of the 1790s.

By the late 1780s Henry Grattan's campaign for parliamentary reform had largely fizzled out. The outbreak of the French Revolution in 1789 brought rejuvenated calls for the introduction of measures to grant Catholics equal representation in parliament. Radicals such as Theobald Wolfe Tone and Samuel Neilson began to discuss the prospect of pushing for political objectives through an organization that included northern Presbyterian dissenters and disaffected Catholics. By 1791, Tone and Neilson, with others such as Thomas Russell and Napper Tandy, had founded the Society of United Irishmen. The organization aimed to unite Catholic, Protestant and Dissenter in the cause of reform. Their objectives, and the radical methods they employed, brought them into conflict with government more than any previous group that had pressed for reform. When a Catholic Convention was called in support of reform in December 1792, political opponents of Catholic reform and Protestant extremists became alarmed. The Convention demanded Catholic emancipation and began a widespread petition campaign. For many, signing the petition was their first political act, and an act that engendered an unprecedented political consciousness. Fervent opposition from conservative quarters emerged and set the scene for the struggle between the reactionaries and the radicals for the remainder of the decade.[67]

The first indication that radical ideas had reached Rathcoole was when John Clinch, of Rathcoole House, became a member of the Society of United Irishmen on 16 March 1792 at just 13 years of age. He was proposed by a Mr Rainsford (possibly the 'Thomas Ransford' noted above as having owned the inn in Rathcoole) and Mr Aylward and was brought before the society at the Music Hall, on Fishamble Street in Dublin, where he was sworn in with around forty members of different religious backgrounds present.[68] Contemporaries took note of the youthful character of these radical political organizations. The rise of the Defenders in the early 1790s through the channels of Dublin's philanthropic societies had prompted Lord Kilwarden to refer to 'clubs of beardless urchins discussing politics and religion'.[69] The Clinch family were the primary minor-gentry figures in the locality around the year 1779 and up until the time of the rebellion. The family lived in Rathcoole House (fig. 4), a Georgian structure situated on the main road next to the church at the eastern end of the village. The Clinchs were an old Catholic family with ties to Newcastle which dated back centuries. They owned extensive property at Hazelhatch as well as a house in the city.[70] Providing further evidence of the family's status, one of the Clinch sons was a distinguished actor and had gained considerable popularity in Dublin in the early 1790s.[71] According to Musgrave, John Clinch was the son of a man of considerable wealth and had received some education. In the period leading up to the 1798 rebellion Clinch sought to be elected a captain in the rebel corps of Rathcoole but was unlucky in that the other main contender was the brother of Felix Rourke, Bryan Rourke. Felix Rourke's influence was such within the United Irishmen that he saw to it that his brother was chosen for the position. Clinch was not to be deterred and owing to his enthusiasm was happy to stay on and serve with the lower rank of sergeant of the Rathcoole corps.[72] It seems clear that Clinch had an impact in politicizing Rathcoole's inhabitants and he may even have convinced Rourke, who would go on to act as a colonel of the Kildare United Irishmen, to join the society.

Who, then, were the forces that sought to suppress radicals such as Clinch? The militia, for one, played a lead role in countering the United Irishmen. In 1793, attempts by government to forcibly enlist Irish men into the ranks of the militia in response to the outbreak of war with France were met with widespread violence and the populace was further politicized. The riots against this imposition signalled a new departure for their violent nature, which included both a willingness by rioters to fire on regular soldiers and an increasingly harsh response by the troops. This, in turn, led to the demise of the moral economy – which had seen the ruled express deference to the ruler – and ultimately created an atmosphere in which the 1798 rebellion was made possible. However, Dublin city and county had remained generally tranquil, the Dublin militia having been filled with substitute English soldiers while many of those balloted had simply vanished into the city's anonymity.[73] In Rathcoole and Newcastle around the time of the rising there were detachments of militia from outside the area such as the Armagh militia. The most prominent local militia force, known as the Uppercross Fusiliers, was under the command of Captain John Finlay.[74] Finlay, who sat as MP, 1790–7, lived to the north-east of Rathcoole at Corkagh Demesne. His father, Thomas Finlay, had purchased the house and estate there in 1750. As lieutenant colonel of the Uppercross Fusiliers, Finlay was charged with the task of suppressing the rebellion in the Clondalkin and Rathcoole area during 1798.[75]

As the United Irishmen continued to expand during the middle of the 1790s, especially in Ulster, the Dublin Castle administration became more and more

4. Rathcoole House

anxious. The Orange Order, representative of the extreme Protestant faction and founded following a skirmish with Catholics in south Armagh in 1795, was soon enlisted as a counter-revolutionary force.[76] The Irish militia was comprised mainly of Catholics at rank-and-file level and was therefore, in the eyes of the government, liable to infiltration. To compound matters, the fencible regiments brought from Britain from 1795 onwards were considered to be second-rate soldiers. These perceptions prompted calls for a new force and to this end the yeomanry was established. Allan Blackstock has set the embodiment of the yeomanry firmly in the context of the growing military strength of the United Irishmen.[77] The yeomen owed much of their origins to the Irish Volunteers. The Volunteers had been raised in 1777 for the protection of the country after vast numbers of the regular military left to fight in the American Revolutionary War. They took centre stage in pressing for reform throughout the late 18th century but were disbanded in 1793 and replaced by the militia.[78] The first record in the sources relating to the Rathcoole Volunteers was in 1781 when they were called upon to bring to justice two men who had attempted to rape a young woman in the neighbourhood.[79] The Rathcoole Volunteers and their fellow Newcastle Volunteers ranked at the bottom of the list in terms of seniority among the Dublin city and county corps.[80] According to Pádraig Ó Snodaigh, 'the Volunteers are too often seen as the architects and agents of reform, and too seldom placed within the pattern and context of loyal local defence'.[81] It is unsurprising, then, that the yeomanry force, which traced its origins to the Volunteers, was also staunchly loyalist.

Approval was granted for the establishment of the yeomanry by the Dublin Castle authorities in September 1796. Under the overall control of Lord Carhampton, both a cavalry and an infantry corps of yeomen were formed with the remit of policing their own counties. The yeomen did not exclude Catholics, nor were they on the whole an Orange force, but with the local gentry charged with their selection they were a predominantly Church of Ireland force. They would go on to act as the primary force of local counter-revolution in the late 1790s while simultaneously gaining notoriety for their staunch loyalism and casual use of violence.[82] In Rathcoole a corps of yeomen cavalry came under the command of Captain Edward Kennedy at Johnstown House. In addition to the cavalry, a corps of infantry yeomen stationed at Rathcoole, and under the command of Lieutenant Charles Ormsby and his brother Captain James Ormsby, bolstered the forces ranged against the rebels.[83] That two brothers enlisted fits a wider pattern documented by Ó Snodaigh who, having examined the muster rolls for yeomanry in counties Roscommon and Wexford, concluded that within the officer ranks of these forces kinship ties were important.[84] The volunteers, militia and yeomen fulfilled the role of policing the locality. Crucially, their leaders were drawn entirely from among the local gentry. By their very presence, and their displays of force through military parades and gatherings, they preserved the social position of the Protestant Ascendancy in the locality while simultaneously alienating much of the Catholic population from the state.

In 1795 vast swathes of the country, including north Kildare, were in a state of great agitation owing to the activities of the Defenders. Agrarian disturbances had been a constant feature of the 18th-century Irish landscape with groups such as the Whiteboys, Hearts of Steel and the Right Boys prepared to use violence to redress socio-economic grievances. The militant Catholic Defenders had grown out of the sectarian tensions and economically competitive climate of mid and south Ulster, but in south Meath and north Kildare they focussed on attaining some form of social justice. The levelling sentiments espoused in court by Laurence O'Connor of Kilcock, one of the few Defender leaders to be tried during this period, were testament to this.[85] Nearly 12 miles from Rathcoole, the village of Kilcock represented the epicentre of Defender activity in north Kildare. The Defenders also thrived a short distance away in Dublin city, making inroads with the personnel of the manufacturing sectors and artisan Jacobin clubs there.[86] In the summer of 1795 they were stated to have 'very lately risen in the counties of … Kildare and Dublin.'[87] Moreover, it is clear from Ciarán Priestley's work on Clonsilla during the 1790s that the Defenders were active in west Co. Dublin at Lucan.[88] Though travelling emissaries often undertook to organize Defender cells outside of their strongholds it appears that no reports of activity by the oath bound society were ever made concerning Rathcoole. The only action attributed to the Defenders in the area occurred in August 1795 when, at the peak of their strength in Kildare, a Mr Nugent, a magistrate in both Kildare and Meath, escorted a suspected sergeant of the Defenders for trial up from the country to Dublin and an attempt was made to rescue the man in Rathcoole.[89]

As near to Rathcoole as both Lucan and Kilcock are, it seems that the Defenders' organizational advance south stalled just short of the village. The slowing of the secret society's expansion may be attributed to two factors. The first of these is a simple matter of distance. In a pre-railway era Rathcoole's distance from the Ulster borderlands epicentre of Defenderism may well have hindered the spread of Defender networks to the locality. The Defenders failed to penetrate as far south as Wicklow or Wexford. Therefore, it is not too presumptuous to conclude that the area to the north of Rathcoole running roughly parallel to the Grand Canal represented the frontier of Defenderism, beyond which the spread of its networks did not manifest in any significant way. Second, there were no major landowners in Rathcoole who were so utterly despised that they could breed tensions which would explode in violence. Chambers, in his study of United Irish and Defender activity in Co. Kildare, has firmly identified Defender motivations as having been agrarian in origin. Their targets were the landlords in the north of the county.[90] As Priestley has explained of Clonsilla, events around the time of the Defender insurgency in 1795 were 'indicative of acute social tension within the locality', events which were almost entirely influenced by the residency of the much-maligned landlord Henry Lawes Luttrell.[91] In light of these conclusions, and the aforementioned absence of influential advocates for reform in the village, it may be surmised that it was the efforts of United Irishmen, rather than those of Defenders or Catholic reformist agitators, which succeeded in raising the class and national consciousness of Rathcoole's inhabitants in the lead up to 1798.

Nationally, the resistance encountered by those who sought to grant some measure of Catholic reform pushed the United Irishmen further towards revolution from 1795. That year Lord Fitzwilliam, the Whig lord lieutenant, attempted to introduce measures for Catholic emancipation but met with opposition from the ascendancy and the extreme Protestant faction in Dublin Castle. Fitzwilliam's subsequent recall saw the more radical members of the Catholic Committee in Dublin practically merge with the United Irishmen. Lord Camden, who replaced Fitzwilliam as lord lieutenant, bolstered the hand of the reactionary elements in the Castle and set the scene for the intense repression of the years that followed.[92] Following the episode, the United Irishmen were left in no doubt as to the need for an armed conspiracy to achieve their goals. Lord Carhampton's brutal repression of the Defenders in Connacht, and the trials and subsequent execution of the organization's leaders in Dublin and elsewhere, meant that by 1796 Defenderism was seriously weakened. In the counties where Defenders had been prevalent, such as Meath and Kildare, they formalized their association with the ever-expanding United Irish cells. However, in 1796, in the southern counties of Leinster and areas around the Wicklow/Dublin border such as Rathcoole where Defenderism had not existed, United Irish membership was yet to rise noticeably.[93]

The same year, 1796, Wolfe Tone was selected by fellow United Irishmen in exile in Philadelphia as emissary to seek military assistance from the French. By December, a French expedition of some 12,000 men under the command of Lazare Hoche had set sail for Ireland. During their attempt to land at

Bantry Bay, violent Atlantic storms sank a number of ships, and, always wary of interception by the British Royal Navy, the French fleet turned back. Although the expedition had failed, morale was raised within United Irish cells across the country as there was now an assurance of an alliance with the French army. United Irish propagandists went into overdrive to spread word about this boon. Loyalists, on the other hand, were horrified by the news of French assistance. The draconian policies adopted by government in response to these developments significantly increased the likelihood of insurrection.[94] In west Cork, for example, General Moore, who was charged with carrying out a campaign of suppression and disarmament of the civilian population, admitted that his orders were 'to treat the people with as much harshness as possible'.[95]

Rumour of Orange bloodlust and the campaign of repression, or 'white terror' as it came to be known, certainly drove many among the peasantry towards rebellion. But there were also other long standing socio-economic grievances that helped mobilize cottiers, labourers and small farmers into the rebel ranks. These included rents, tithes, evictions, agricultural prices and lack of employment. An additional major economic grievance held by the peasantry in the lead up to the 1798 rebellion, as Dickson has demonstrated, was the burden of various taxes. The English war with the French from 1793 led to a shortfall in the exchequer. Government moved to impose heavier duties on salt and it withdrew subsidies on inland and coastal carriage of grain to Dublin, while taxes on leather and tobacco were also increased and impacted upon rural dwellers.[96] As Smyth has noted, United Irish ideology was often contradictory. Its pamphlets contained a social-radicalism, best embodied by Thomas Russell and Jemmy Hope, which sat side by side with a bourgeois conservative attitude, represented by moderate figures in the society such as W.J. MacNevin, who feared placing power with the masses. On the whole, issues of social injustice were secondary to those of radical political reform; but if they were, the levelling principles contained in United Irish propaganda helped to enlist the popular support of the peasantry who were more concerned with their immediate survival.[97]

Such popular support for the United Irish cause only appeared quite late in the day in some counties. Daniel Gahan has documented how a period of relative quiet existed in Co. Wexford in the middle of the decade, until the expansion of the United Irish cell structure in the county from 1797 onward. The growth of the organization occurred in a steady progression of organizing 'a parish at a time, a barony at a time, until it was well established among ... liberal Protestants and Catholics of north Leinster'.[98] As in Wexford, the majority of Rathcoole's inhabitants who took part in the rising only appear to have been brought into the United Irish cell structure during the peak of its expansion in Leinster in late 1797 and early 1798. This spread was aided by a new constitution, which had been adopted in August 1797 to alter the framework of leadership within the organization in an attempt to make it more amenable to military structures. Tommy Graham maintains that the Leinster United Irish comeback during this period meant that 'not only was organization consolidated and membership increased in existing strongholds such as Dublin, Meath and Kildare, but it was successfully extended into Wicklow, Carlow and Wexford.'[99]

The importance of Dublin at this time as a hub for disseminating revolutionary doctrine cannot be underestimated. Following General Lake's campaign of repression throughout 1797, which had left the northern United Irish structures in tatters, Dublin overtook Belfast as the principal centre for the distribution of propaganda. From their base in Dublin, United Irish recruiting sergeants, organizers and agents carrying radical doctrine were sent forth into the countryside to politicize the minds of the disaffected.[100] Taking into account its position on the main road to Kilkenny and beyond that to Munster, Rathcoole would have been frequented regularly by such emissaries, providing them with ample opportunity to convey United Irish ideology to the local population. Further to the west and south in Leinster magistrates' reports during 1797 from Sallins, Co. Kildare, and Baltinglass, Co. Wicklow, 10 and 25 miles from Rathcoole respectively, indicated that print had been circulated widely and imbibed by the lower classes there.[101] In January 1798, William Clancy, a government supporter and native of Ballymount near Rathcoole, remarked on the spread of the printed word in the area in correspondence with his brother James who lived in London. He claimed that *The Press*, the organ of the United Irishmen, which he slandered as a 'vile republican paper', was sold by a man named Moore in the area and printed with such regularity and haste that 'a great number of mistakes are committed'. The organ was deemed seditious by the administration and William's father forbade him send a copy to his brother, who held United Irish sympathies, regarding all who subscribed to the paper as marked men.[102] Though there is no extant documentary evidence for the distribution of print in Rathcoole itself, it seems clear that the village was similarly inundated with republican newspapers, ballads, handbills, manifestos and pamphlets from at least 1797, if not earlier.

As noted previously, the majority of Rathcoole's populace were only partially literate. However, quite likely above half could read to some degree and most were proficient in English. Kevin Whelan has documented how the United Irishmen's 'recourse to the printed word had the effect of concentrating its most effective penetration in Anglophone and literate areas, which had close links to the main publishing centres of the period, Dublin and Belfast'.[103] The United Irishmen had a sufficient cohort of readers in Rathcoole who could engage with publications such as *The Press*. For those unable to read, local leaders such as John Clinch and Felix Rourke could convey the United Irish literature that had been sent to Rathcoole from the capital and thus garner support for the republican cause. Ó Cíosáin has described this practice of 'reading aloud', which was central to United Irish politicization, as having occurred in both a 'vertical' fashion, where those reading conveyed the social superiority of the literate, and in 'horizontal' form, where reading took place among equals.[104]

E.P. Thompson has also noted this practice in late-18th and early 19th-century England whereby 'very few of the working people can read well enough to read a newspaper; although papers are taken (and read aloud) at the blacksmith's, the barber's and … public houses.'[105]

The effect on the locality of this spread in literature, coupled with the barely detectable conspiratorial organizational work of the United Irish cells, was a rise in house attacks with the aim of acquiring arms. Attacks by what the papers described as 'armed villains' had occurred in both Rathcoole and the wider Co. Dublin area during the late 1780s.[106] Near Tallaght Hill in 1788, a gang robbed a carman's inn of butter, bacon and fowl, 'terrifying with horrid imprecations the landlord and his wife, as well as several people put up there'.[107] Earlier, in 1784 at Rathcoole, three highwaymen with their faces blackened robbed a young lady and her servant of 24 guineas and a horse. The *Freeman's Journal* decried the 'various depredations … committed on the Naas road, which render it highly dangerous to travellers'.[108] However, the first reported signs of rebel activity in Rathcoole took place four months after Bantry in April 1797 when a nocturnal raid was carried out on the house of a Mr Simpson in the village. A party of close to 200 rebels forced in the door of the house and made off with two fowling pieces. On the same night, five miles away at Celbridge, *The Times* reported that a group of 'marauders', who had carried out similar actions on previous nights, stripped the house of Mr Tisdall of its arms.[109]

The newspapers of the day failed to make a connection between the expanding United Irish structures and these raids. The attacks were downplayed, either because the papers were unaware of United Irish activity on the ground or because they wished to brand the soon-to-be rebels as 'banditti', 'plunderers' and 'freebooters' for propaganda purposes. There existed the possibility that house raids were undertaken as the unsettled state of the country provided a pretext for arms acquisition by the peasantry. That this activity coincided with reports of drilling and increased United Irish expansion, however, points towards the raids having had political and military objectives.[110] The character and objectives of the attacks evolved as rebellion approached. Those that took place during the 1780s, though indicative of poverty induced crime and social tension, usually only involved several robbers and were not focussed on acquiring arms. The raids which occurred from 1797 onwards were distinguishable from the smaller incidents which preceded them in that large militant bands of rebels sought out weaponry specifically.

The experiences of the abovementioned Clancy family of Ballymount, five miles north-east along the high road from Rathcoole, sheds light on both the changing attitudes of local residents during these turbulent years and the detail of the house raids, which became more frequent from 1797. The Protestant family possessed a degree of wealth: they lived in a two-storey home where they employed a team of servants; they owned another residence in the city; could afford medicines; and they owned a horse for the purpose of hunting.

They exchanged a series of illuminating private letters that spanned the years 1797–9.[111] Politically, the head of the household, Patrick, was a moderate and supporter of Henry Grattan.[112] Patrick did not blindly defend the military when in late 1797 they clashed with republicans in the Theatre Royal in Dublin. The republicans had called for a patriotic tune to be sung, which prompted the military men present to attempt to force the patrons to remove their hats and stand for 'God save the king', causing a riot in which three lives were lost.[113]

Another son of the family, James Clancy, had left Ireland for London at some point in the 1790s. His brother wrote to him in August 1797 describing a house raid in which the Clancys were targeted and stated that such attacks were becoming more common in the neighbourhood. A group of what he branded 'Defenders', which included a number of women, surrounded the Clancy home in the middle of the night and broke in. They fired shots through the window and used an improvised device known as a 'swivel sledge' in an attempt to gain entry, which according to William 'few doors could resist'. Despite William's efforts at deterring the raiders by brandishing his blunderbuss from the top window, the raiders made off with a number of arms and 12 guineas, which William handed to them after realizing resistance was futile. Demonstrating the presence of a levelling mind-set, the party demanded the guns be handed across at the front door rather than being thrown down to them from the second storey 'as if they were dogs'. They apparently knew what weapons were in the house, and where they were stored, as they made specific demands of the occupants for the brass-barrelled pistols they kept upstairs. Such inside knowledge signified that one of the Clancys' several servants had passed on the location of the weapons to them. This episode is indicative of the, at times, very personal nature of the rising. Servants and labourers who worked on farms for middle- or upper-class landowners such as the Clancys quite likely harboured a resentment beneath the surface that they had an opportunity to express during these years of strife. William's cousin had also been in the house at the time of the raid and his political opinions were transformed in its aftermath. Prior to the raid their cousin had been of a liberal persuasion, an opponent of the incumbent government and therefore probably in favour of granting Catholic reform. He later became an ardent supporter of government policy and according to William 'turned against Defenderism and vomited all his old principles since that affair'.[114]

A month or so later in mid-September another incident took place where a house, this time belonging to Mr Sleater of Rathcoole, was surrounded by more than 100 rebels who demanded that any arms which were inside be given up to them. They managed to make off with a musket, a fowling piece and a number of pistols. On leaving the village they passed by Newlands, Clondalkin, and fired a volley of shots at the door of a wealthy farmer's house, one Lawrence Rourke. The *Freeman's Journal* reported that this was a retaliatory attack by the band for having faced resistance while raiding for arms there a number of days previously.[115] The growing number of similar incidents of house raids in the area prompted the government to post a detachment of infantry at Rathcoole in the closing days of September 1797. A number of cavalry were also charged with patrolling the area at night in order to deter the rebels from conducting raids in the locality.[116] Attacks such as these continued to intensify in the village of Rathcoole and in the wider area, particularly to the south in Wicklow. By October 1797, *The Oracle and Public Advertiser* declared that in Co. Wicklow, previously one of the most tranquil areas in the country, in the last week, there was not a single night 'in which some glaring outrage or robbery has not been perpetrated in the vicinity of Blessington alone'.[117] The same month the *Freeman's Journal* carried a report of a house having been plundered in Saggart by rebels from Crumlin, who upon their capture confessed to a magistrate that they were in possession of 40 pieces of arms, most likely amassed from their recent activities raiding houses in the locality.[118]

Four miles from Rathcoole, in Clondalkin, raids for arms had become so frequent that by the close of 1797 those in the locality who were loyal to government, or wished to protect their homesteads, contacted Dublin Castle to convey their grievances. William Caldbeck, a prominent powder mill owner in Clondalkin, wrote to Chief Secretary Thomas Pelham on 10 November 1797 to state that there had been 'many robberies lately committed in that part of the county upon poor as well as rich, taking their provisions, apparel and furniture'. Caldbeck requested permission to form an association of men to conduct patrols in the area in order to combat the ongoing raids. To this end he suggested 'that five or eight of the most substantial shall be chosen and sworn constables and that one of them acting as sergeant shall lead a mighty guard and patrol round'. Attached to his letter were the names of 43 signatories, mostly farmers, who had signed their names in the hopes of strengthening the request. Pelham ultimately rejected Caldbeck's proposed association and instead opted for additional troops to be stationed in the area.[119]

The situation continued to escalate from the start of 1798. In January, Patrick Clancy, the head of his household at Ballymount, wrote to his son James in London and stated that fourteen 'boys', one of whom previously worked for him, from the Ballymount area and nearby Red Cow, had been sent to Kilmainham to await trial for robbery and burglary including that of his own home the previous summer. An informant from among the group by the name of Keogh, who had worked for Patrick Clancy – again emphasizing the personal nature of the attack on the Clancy home – gave evidence that the arms found upon the capture of these men were those that were taken from the Clancys on the night of the raid. James Reilly was later tried and found guilty of the robbery. William Clancy noted that his brother had a 'prophetic tongue [which] often allotted that man [Reilly] for the gallows', confirming that the Clancys were indeed well-acquainted with those who had raided their home. By early January 1798 Patrick Clancy remarked that 'the situation of this country is truly alarming and not at all exaggerated'.[120]

5. Felix Rourke

On 25 January 1798 William wrote that 'murder is scarce looked upon as a matter of much consequence, we are so accustomed to it' and that 'the people of this part of the country are so changed you'd scarce know them to be the same people'. William had been present at a number of riots at Stephen's Green in Dublin where republicans had clashed with the military and he claimed he was nearly killed 'twice or thrice by the advocates of liberty'. However, he also condemned the instances of government repression that he had heard of including the military firing on suspected republican prisoners while they were confined in a tender and cramming others into a plague infested gaol.[121] William's comment regarding the change in people illustrates in particular the mind-set of local pro-government supporters who witnessed their neighbours take up arms for the rebel cause, and, in their eyes, against them personally. James Kelly's work on the experience of Irish Protestants during the course of the rebellion demonstrates how their interpretation of history had at its centre the perceived massacre of their ancestors during a previous period of insurrection in 1641.[122] The raid on their home and the continuing violence in the locality caused significant unease for the Church of Ireland Clancys as they believed the threat of such massacre had been brought to their very doorstep.

During the early months of 1798 a key United Irish figure from Rathcoole, Felix Rourke (fig. 5), emerges in the sources. Over the course of the next five years Rourke would become the village's most active and senior United Irishman. Madden described Rourke as having been, at the beginning of 1798, 'a very young man, of great zeal in the cause'.[123] Rourke was born in 1765 to a small farmer who kept a turnpike gate and operated a carman's stage between Rathcoole and Naas at Blackchurch. The Rourkes lived at Broadfield about a half a mile from Rathcoole. After completing an apprenticeship in Dublin as a shoemaker, and later having been employed as a clerk, Felix Rourke returned to assist his father on their small farm. It is not known when he was first sworn in as a United Irishman, but in the spring of 1798 his activities earned him the attention of the society's leaders. He earned the trust and confidence of Lord Edward FitzGerald who demonstrated his friendship to Rourke when he presented him with a gift of his favourite mare shortly before the outbreak of the rebellion.[124] Rourke also knew another prominent United Irishman, Samuel Neilson, on a personal basis, referring to him as the 'noble-minded editor of *The Northern Star*'. These connections underscore Rourke's ties to high-ranking United Irish figures and his status within the organization.[125] Unlike the majority of United Irishmen, who were excluded through a vetting process,[126] Rourke was also a member of the yeomanry. He was a permanent sergeant in the Rathcoole yeomanry under the leadership of Lieutenant Charles Ormsby.[127] Rourke seems to have cut off all ties with Ormsby at the beginning of 1798, around the same time Lord Edward FitzGerald entrusted him with being in charge of the rebels' organizational endeavours in the Rathcoole area.[128] His brother, Charles Rourke, also a yeoman, would defer deserting from the Rathcoole cavalry until the beginning of the rebellion.[129] Felix Rourke's friend and fellow leader in the area, Bartholomew Mahon, was made secretary of the Barony of Newcastle at the same time. Rourke was then appointed to the same post for the Barony of Upper Cross. Felix Rourke's father was also suspected by Ormsby of having been on the baronial committee.[130] Both Rourke and Mahon went on to attain the office of county delegates. Sometime after that Lord Edward FitzGerald appointed Rourke as a colonel in the Kildare United Irishmen, a move that meant he was not actually involved in events at Rathcoole during the rebellion.[131]

During the spring of 1798, United Irish organization in Rathcoole continued apace. An unnamed informant who had risen to the level of captain in Lucan described a secret assembly to elect leaders in the area:

> I was brought to a meeting at Saggard by Philip Geraty where several met whose names I don't recollect, except one Lyons of Newcastle, who's Christian name I don't know … also the miller of Saggard whose name is Masterson & one Keely who is a yeoman in the Rathfarnham core of cavalry.[132]

Rebel plans were dealt a crushing blow upon the arrest of most of Leinster's key leaders by a troop under the command of spymaster Major Sirr at Oliver Bond's house on 12 March 1798. Alluding to the arrests and widespread repression, Patrick Clancy of Ballymount described Dublin as 'a town in the state of siege'.[133]

Despite the charismatic Lord Edward FitzGerald having initially managed to remain at large, within a number of weeks he too was in government custody. In the wake of the arrests at Bond's a number of the Kildare committees met to determine who had betrayed their society to government. Rourke was forced to defend himself against an accusation by Tom Reynolds, who was later revealed to be the actual informant guilty of betraying Bond and the other leaders. Rourke's life was in grave danger but the society made inquiries and found the charges unsubstantiated and subsequently allowed him to walk free. His close friend, Bartholomew Mahon, believed this incident was an ordeal for Rourke and the only time he had ever seen the Rathcoole man in such an agitated state that he was brought to tears.[134]

On 13 March 1798, Rourke was involved in the first act of fatal violence in Rathcoole prior to the outbreak of rebellion. That evening Mr Buckley, Rathcoole's largest landowner, was on his way back home from the city when some locals encouraged him to drink in Doyle's public house in the village until late at night. Buckley's body was afterwards found near Rourke's house at Broadfield. Charles Ormsby believed Buckley was killed as he was a known loyalist, but his position as the largest landowner in Rathcoole may also have led to his assassination. When Ormsby came upon the slain Buckley he identified a bayonet belonging to his Rathcoole infantry protruding from his body. At this point Ormsby ordered that the yeomen under his command assemble on parade so that he might ascertain who Buckley's killer was by identifying any man whose bayonet was missing. All the yeomen had their bayonets and Rourke never showed up for the parade and so was suspected of the killing. Ormsby searched for Rourke for some time, calling up to his family home only to receive vague excuses from Rourke's father regarding his son's whereabouts.[135] It later emerged that four of the corps, quite likely including Rourke, were involved in Buckley's killing and that John Clinch, who had access to the arms store, replaced the bayonet that the assassins had left lodged in Buckley's body.[136]

As rebellion drew nearer an anonymous informant from the Rathcoole area reported a spate of attacks and robberies, including Buckley's killing, in the neighbourhood in mid-March 1798. He wrote that a Mr Nolan's home was attacked, as was a Mr Parivol's on the same night with the intention of killing the latter, while 'another man was cut to pieces near Newcastle'. The informant also reported 'persons exercising intentionally at night in the Commons of Saggart'.[137] On 16 and 17 March it was reported that a Mr Morgan, a Mr Lyons and others in the Rathcoole area were robbed of arms.[138] A fortnight later another violent attack without the obvious aim of acquiring arms took place for the second time in the neighbourhood. A gentleman travelling on horseback along the road near Rathcoole village was shot at by a pair described in reports of the time as 'ruffians'. The gentleman narrowly escaped, the bullet grazing the side of his head. The yeomanry later came across the pair in a cabin and apprehended them.[139] It appears that some rebels, many of whom would have harboured personal resentments towards their social superiors who extracted rents from them, sensed that control was slipping away from the state and seized the opportunity to attack landowning and gentry figures such as Buckley and the unnamed gentleman.

In early 1798, personal and class-based antipathies continued to permeate at the local level as the country became more turbulent. The intensification of attacks in the area saw William Clancy of Ballymount join the local yeomanry in early April. He was led to state that all he could expect in the papers was news of 'conflagrations and murders'.[140] William, despite his increasingly reactionary outlook, maintained correspondence with his brother James in London, a United Irish sympathizer, and continued to send him the republican *Press*, pleading with his brother to make contact and let him know he was safe.[141] He later described both the Castle and the gaols as having been crowded with prisoners. The gulf between the forces of reaction and radicalism in the neighbourhood continued to widen. Demonstrating the localized and apparently factional nature of these grander political clashes once again, Clancy remarked that 'there are two parties called the Crops and the Tails who are fighting every night. The Crops have instruments for cutting tails, and the tails have pitch caps to put on Crops ... so between them careful men like me are afraid to venture out after nightfall'.[142]

In the weeks immediately preceding the rebellion, James Ormsby, captain of the Rathcoole yeomanry and brother to Lieutenant Charles Ormsby, wrote to Edward Cooke on 7 May to inform him that the rebels had been organizing in the area. He alleged that large quantities of pikes were hidden in the chapel at Newcastle and in the loft of the adjoining house. He recommended that the villages of Saggart and Newcastle be searched for arms. Ormsby, displaying an anti-Catholic bias, specifically singled out the Catholic priest Fr James Harold's house in Rathcoole for attention despite there having been little evidence to suggest the cleric had become radicalized. Ormsby stated that the rebels in the area were resolute and, referring to the violent measures government had employed to frustrate United Irish organization in the neighbouring county, he wrote that they 'expect the same treatment their friends have met with in the County of Kildare'.[143] Ormsby's pronouncement was significant as it illustrated a number of important realities. First, that even at this late stage 'white terror' had not been visited on Rathcoole. Second, that the rebels expected violent repression, a fact that may have driven more locals into the rebel ranks through fear. And third, that those rebels who had already nailed their colours to the mast were determined to do battle. During these final weeks of preparation for rebellion John Clinch began to organize the surrounding neighbourhood with greater fervour. Clinch was acting on instructions issued in April from the Leinster command that specified how each county was to be readied for imminent war. Rebel leaders began to meet regularly at his home, Rathcoole House, in order to orchestrate the rebellion in the area.[144]

2. The 1798 Rebellion in Rathcoole

Throughout the month of May 1798 what remained of the United Irish Leinster leadership began to develop plans for a Dublin-focused rebellion that would be conducted without French military assistance. The intended rising was to unfold in three phases. The first phase was to ensure that the rebels in Dublin would take and hold key positions throughout the city with support coming from Co. Dublin into the city. The second phase involved counties such as Kildare, Meath and Wicklow where rebels were to take positions that would nullify the threat of an immediate counterattack on the city by the military garrisons stationed there. After accomplishing this they were then to march on Dublin upon receiving word that the rising in the city had begun. The final phase entailed stopping the mail coaches that ran from Dublin to Munster, Connacht, Ulster and the remainder of Leinster, which would act as a signal to the rest of the country to rise and also prevent local crown forces from reaching the capital. After Lord Edward FitzGerald's arrest on 19 May planning for the rising was left in the hands of Samuel Neilson. Neilson believed that the lack of strong leadership was a major weakness, and, on the night of 23 May, he was arrested in an attempt to free the imprisoned leaders from Newgate prison. The city was now without any of its primary leaders. Informants had also passed details of the rebels' intended assembly points in Dublin to government and, as a result, thousands of yeomen were posted in areas such as Smithfield and Newmarket, while the Liffey bridges were barricaded and citywide checkpoints were established. The rising in Dublin city had been foiled.[1]

In Rathcoole, the rebels, working in concert with their comrades in Dublin, had planned to attack the local garrison on the night of 23 May. Musgrave remarked that 'a yeoman officer, and a magistrate, who patrolled the country for four miles round Rathcoole in the county of Dublin, assured me, that he did not find a single man but one in above a hundred cabins and farm-houses, which he searched for arms, the night before the rebellion broke out; their inmates having assembled, in order to concert measures for the general insurrection'.[2] The Rathcoole military garrison, which consisted of 43 privates and three officers, was to come under assault at the same time as Kildare United Irishmen kept government forces in the countryside west of Rathcoole occupied by mounting their own offensives. The attempt on Rathcoole also hinged on the infiltration of the local yeomanry corps and the assassination of Lieutenant Ormsby and his brother Captain James Ormsby. Having killed the corps' leaders, the infiltrators were to immediately join the rebel forces and assume the attack on Rathcoole. However, the plan to assassinate the Ormsbys did not come to fruition as the initial attack on the village was foiled by a number of the Armagh militia who were stationed in both Rathcoole and Newcastle and a detachment of Rathcoole cavalry under the command of Captain Edward Kennedy. Government forces were well aware of the rebels' intended assault on the village as, for a number of nights prior to the intended attack, they had witnessed United Irishmen drilling on the hills of Redgap and Coolmine that overlook the village. General Lake was informed of the imminent rebel offensive on Rathcoole and, after taking into account the village's strategic importance and understrength garrison, he despatched reinforcements numbering 80 Scottish fencibles under the command of the experienced Colonel Hunter, a move that ended rebel hopes of mounting a successful surprise attack on the village's crown forces. It remains unclear as to why the rebels were discouraged from attacking a garrison that, even with reinforcements, amounted to no more than 150. Musgrave claimed that up to 3,000 rebels had gathered on the hills overlooking Rathcoole village in lieu of the planned attack.[3] Although this was no doubt an exaggerated claim, if only a fifth of that figure materialized and were ready to descend on Rathcoole they might have caused problems for the garrison stationed there.

Having forestalled the rebel attack on Rathcoole through the strategic deployment of reinforcements, government forces in the village then went on the offensive. The favourable situation Lieutenant Ormsby found himself in inspired him to venture into the hitherto off-limits hills. The garrison of the town was short on provisions due to their increased number and Ormsby consequently took a body of men to the high ground above the village to forage. In pursuit of their supplies the yeomen came across a young shepherd boy who was known to watch a flock on the hills. Violence was used on the boy in an effort to extract information from him regarding the whereabouts of the rebels who had been seen on the hills in the previous days. After Ormsby struck him a number of times he pointed out John Shea and his brother Pat who were both privates in the yeomanry corps.[4] The rebel plot to kill the Ormsbys subsequently came apart with the names of the remaining conspirators soon becoming known to their intended targets. Sergeant John Walsh along with corporals Dillon, Byrne and Harvey were revealed as conspirators in the plot and as members of Rathcoole's United Irish leadership.[5]

Rebel contingents had more fortune in assembling at other locations in Dublin's rural hinterland. On 23 May a large band of rebels, estimated at about 500, gathered eight miles to the east of Rathcoole, at Rathfarnham.[6] The group split into two detachments, with one heading northwards to Clondalkin and the other taking a western route through Tallaght and on to Rathcoole. There were already a number of rebel bands waiting to move into the city along many of the roads directly to its south at places like Dalkey, Booterstown, Donnybrook and Harold's Cross.[7] Therefore, the detachment sent to Clondalkin may have been attempting to take up a strategic position in order to have the rebel contingents approaching Dublin from a more south-westerly direction and on as many roads as possible when the signal was given for their advance to begin. The rebels who had risen at Rathfarnham and made for Rathcoole may have sought to link up with those who had planned to take the strategically important village and then also move on Dublin in accordance with the aforementioned second phase of the United Irish strategy to take the city.

The rebels who had been dispatched to Clondalkin reached their destination early on 24 May. In their command were two men known only by their surnames, Ledwich and Wade, both of whom had deserted from Lord Ely's corps of Rathfarnham yeomanry.[8] The rebels had first made their way to Crumlin nearer to the city but had found none of their comrades on the commons there as they had expected to. They instead turned back south for the commons of Clondalkin, according to *The Times*, 'with four or five carts loaded … with blankets, provisions, powder and ball'. Ledwich and Wade scouted the road ahead for government forces. When they returned – demonstrating a lack of military discipline – the pair ordered the rebels to disband as soldiers under Colonel Finlay were approaching. The majority of the rebels managed to escape through nearby fields and ditches, but some of their number remained on the road and were caught by the dragoons who killed two and captured Ledwich and another high-ranking rebel, Edward Keogh, after seriously wounding him.[9] Both were taken to the Castle, tried by court-martial and hanged.[10] The two rebels who had been killed were James Keely and James Byrne. Keely had also been a member of the Rathfarnham yeomanry and had been organizing in Saggart before the rebellion.[11] Their bodies were taken to Dublin by Colonel Finlay and hung from a bridge over the Liffey as a warning to the public.[12]

The second rebel detachment that made its way to Rathcoole, despite also facing difficult circumstances, fared slightly better in that they managed to make a stand against the crown forces. Lord Camden had received intelligence that the rebels had risen in Rathfarnham and immediately ordered a detachment of the 5th dragoons under Lieutenant O'Reilly to be dispatched to engage them. Assisted by the earl of Roden and Lieutenant Colonel Puleston, the crown forces made their way to Rathfarnham, but upon arrival found that the rebels had already left for Rathcoole. On their way the rebel force attacked a group of yeoman cavalry, forcing them to retreat. The United Irishmen proceeded to raise the standard of rebellion, with the words *Erin go Bragh* emblazoned on it, on the commons at Saggart.[13] They did not celebrate their victory for long as government forces under O'Reilly had met the fleeing yeomen on the road who advised the commander of the rebels' position on the commons. O'Reilly devised a pincer movement that saw him take one body of troops and Roden the other in an effort to outflank the rebels. A clash ensued and O'Reilly's force drove the rebels back from Brown's Barn toward the waiting Roden who had manoeuvred behind them and onto the commons at Saggart.[14] With the government troops now completely surrounding the rebels a small-scale battle ensued. Giving an indication of the conflict's magnitude, the *Express and Evening*

Chronicle later reported that yeomen stationed up to 10 miles away at St Stephen's Green in the city distinctly heard the discharge of weapons during the clash in Saggart.[15] Many of the rebels were mounted and well-armed, but, encircled as they were, they had little hope of repelling the well-trained dragoons. Three rebels were killed and upwards of 30 captured along with a number of pikes and supply carts. The remaining rebels managed to escape into the dense countryside that prohibited the mounted troops from giving chase.[16] As in the aftermath of the clash at Fox and Geese, the bodies of the dead men were brought to the Castle to be put on display, while a horse and a pair of boots belonging to one of the rebels were paraded through the streets of Dublin as trophies.[17]

The defence of the key strategic position along the main road outside Saggart might have succeeded if the rebels from the hills overlooking Rathcoole had taken the village and linked up with their Rathfarnham counterparts approaching from the east. Yet, as Ruán O'Donnell has pointed out, events such as those that transpired at Rathcoole, where the insurgents did not get as far as engaging the crown forces, were not unique. Bands of rebels who had gathered in the greater Dublin area at places such as Tallaght and Dalkey in the south and Artane and Clontarf in the north never clashed with crown forces at all 'owing to the indecision caused by the initial fate of the city men'.[18] Instead, rebels in the south made their way to Blackmore Hill in Wicklow, while those in the north of the city travelled west to the Hill of Tara in Meath where large camps were established. Dublin city had failed to rise and most of the county rebels from surrounding areas such as Rathcoole had either made their way to the rebel camps or accepted pardons. Nevertheless, counties such as Carlow, Kildare, Meath and Wicklow erupted in rebellion after ill-founded rumours of a United Irish victory in Dublin began to circulate, while the burning of mail coaches at Santry in north Dublin and Johnstown near Naas had also provided the signal for many rebels to rise.[19]

In Kildare, the United Irishmen launched attacks on Kilcullen, Clane, Prosperous and Naas early on the morning of 24 May.[20] Felix Rourke was involved in the drive to capture Naas from the Johnstown Road. His brother Bryan Rourke, who like Felix had not been involved in the attempt to take Rathcoole but had been camped at Whelp Rock and Blackmore Hill near Blessington, made his way towards Prosperous as a high-ranking leader of a large rebel contingent.[21] Dr John Esmonde, formerly of the Sallins yeomanry, led the rebel attack on Prosperous village under the cover of darkness. The rebel forces gathered at the canal to the south and from there managed to rush the village's garrison under the command of Captain Swayne, who was taken by surprise and killed as he slept. The rebels locked the remaining soldiers inside the barracks and a number of other buildings and set them ablaze. Many of the soldiers perished in the flames, leapt to their deaths or were killed by rebels as they attempted to flee.[22] Bryan Rourke and the rebels who attacked Prosperous had gained a decisive victory. On the other hand, Felix Rourke, a colonel in the Kildare United men, had met with defeat after an hour-long battle at the heavily fortified garrison town of Naas.[23] A number of rebel victories in Kildare, combined with General Dundas's defensive-minded policy of contraction whereby crown forces retreated to major towns such as Athy and Naas, meant that by 26 May the insurgents controlled vast swathes of Kildare. This was to mark the peak of their campaign. Without Dublin having been taken the Kildare men ran out of momentum and after a number of defeats the rebels gradually took to encamping in remote and easily defended areas such as the Bog of Allen.[24]

As the Kildare rebellion began to noticeably run its course by 26 May, in the south-east Wexford suddenly rose. Early rebel victories in Wexford such as that at Oulart Hill on 27 May boosted United Irish morale across the country and sparked renewed efforts to organize a concerted rising in Antrim and Down. After United Irish victories at Enniscorthy, Gorey and Wexford town, a 'Wexford Republic' was formed so that by the end of May the rebels held most of the county.[25] Of the closing week of May in Co. Dublin Musgrave remarked that 'the roads leading to the metropolis were so completely obstructed by bands of rebels, who roamed through and pillaged the adjacent country that no mail-coach arrived there.' The dispersal of rebels from the main roads out of Dublin by the end of May meant that by early June Co. Dublin had, in most places, returned to relative tranquillity.[26] As open warfare and mass insurrection continued in Wexford, south Dublin and Kildare entered a new phase of rebellion at the beginning of June that was to be characterized less by open battles and more by guerrilla style warfare.

At Rathcoole, in the aftermath of the foiled rebel plan to assassinate Charles Ormsby, John Clinch continued to elude government forces until he was apprehended sometime towards the end of May. Clinch was informed upon by Sergeant John Walsh who had been accused of conspiring to kill Ormsby himself. It later transpired that Walsh had been employed by the government spymaster, Major Sirr, and had infiltrated the Rathcoole United Irish leadership from early on, a fact that probably alerted loyalist forces to the drilling of rebels on the hills in the days before the rising. Walsh passed information to government stating that Clinch had sworn both him and Felix Rourke into the United Irish ranks.[27] After being captured, Clinch was brought to the Provost prison at the Royal barracks where he was court-martialled on 1 June.[28] He wrote his last letter there the following day:

Honoured Father,

I expected to have seen or heard from you ere this. I fear my fate is determined; I am told I am to suffer death this day. It would be a great satisfaction to me to see you before I die; and if you could bring or send a priest to me, I think I could then die happy: at all events, I will meet my fate with fortitude. I would not for worlds exchange situations with

Walsh, my prosecutor, who has behaved in the most base and treacherous manner, and swore to several falsehoods. His charges were as follow: that I swore him to be true to the French, and that I was a sergeant in the rebels, and attended a meeting of Sergeants, to elect a captain. Dear father, I assure you the foregoing charges are false, and, as I hope for salvation, I declared the truth at the court-martial. I hope, dear father, you will bear this with fortitude, and comfort my dear mother on this trying occasion. I feel more for my friends than myself. My love to my dear sisters Swords, Ann, Kitty, Fanny, Alicia, Michael and Larrey and my brother-in-law Swords. As I am preparing for that awful moment, I beg you'll excuse any omission on my side.

I am, honoured father, your ever dutiful and now unfortunate son,

John Clinch.

Provost Prison, June 2, 1798,

Eight o'clock in the morning.[29]

Clinch's attempt to distance himself from the United Irish cause in the hours before his death was perhaps an effort to spare his family the animosity of the local yeomanry. After writing his final letter he was brought to Newgate prison where his execution was to take place. Following his capture, Lord Edward FitzGerald was also held in Newgate and was present during Clinch's execution. FitzGerald was fatally wounded from the altercation that arose when he was arrested at his safe-house on Thomas Street and was in a delirious state, his body at times convulsing. Clinch was then brought up and hanged and his body left swinging from the gallows, prompting the crowd who had gathered to call out for him to be cut down. When one of their number tried to get to the rebel's body a soldier shouted 'don't touch him, damn you, don't touch him' and a shot was fired. The clamour below further unsettled Lord Edward who, remembering his common cause with the executed Clinch, loudly cried out 'God look down on those who suffer! God preserve me and have mercy on me and those that act with me'.[30] In the aftermath of the young rebel's execution, and his father's death shortly afterwards, the Clinch family sold up Rathcoole House.[31] Clinch's execution and the arrest of the parish priest, Fr Harold, were immortalized in the words of the following ballad, passed down through local tradition:

> My curse attend you, east and west,
> My curse attend you night and day,
> You hung John Clinch and sent the priest away.[32]

'East' and 'west' most likely refer to Walsh and Ormsby who were instrumental in having Clinch hanged. Local tradition also has it that Clinch was offered a pardon in return for betraying his comrades but that he replied by declaring 'information I deny. A gentleman I lived, a gentleman I'll die'.[33]

During the course of June the rebellion in Wexford faltered. In Down and Antrim Henry Monro and Henry Joy McCracken led a brief insurgency that was crushed at the battles of Ballynahinch and Antrim.[34] In Kildare the rebel camps, set up at the end of May, continued to affect the stability of the Rathcoole area. Three thousand rebels had also surrendered to General Dundas at Kilcullen at the end of May.[35] Charles Ormsby was incensed by the refusal of Felix Rourke and his Co. Dublin United Irish comrades to surrender at this point.[36] With no intentions of adhering to the General's terms, many, including Rourke, made their way to the camp on Whelp Rock near Blessington and to the hills overlooking Tallaght and Rathcoole. Rourke had already established close ties with United Irishmen to the east of Rathcoole, such as John Mathews of Tallaght Hill whom Madden described as a 'friend and companion' of the Rathcoole man.[37] Rathcoole's strategic importance was again highlighted in mid-June when rebel priest Fr Martin drew up plans – which never came to fruition – to take the village with a force under the command of General Holt. Martin envisaged the rebels descending from the Wicklow mountains and launching an attack on Rathfarnham, Templeogue and Rathcoole before moving on the still exposed Dublin.[38]

With so many rebels within a day's march of Rathcoole, the village and its surrounding countryside remained in a state of disturbance throughout June. The closing days of June were notable for a resurgence in politically motivated activity in Rathcoole. This most likely occurred as a result of rebels returning to the area after the Kildare campaigns launched from the Bog of Allen and Timahoe camps had ceased following crushing defeats for United Irish commanders such as William Aylmer at the battle of Ovidstown on 18 June. On 20 June, a number of the City of Cork Militia, who were based three miles from Rathcoole at Hazelhatch, attempted to bring a prisoner to Sallins in Kildare. Not long after crossing the county border they were attacked by a group of rebels. Lieutenant Elias Pearce who had remained behind at the militia's base dispatched a reinforcement of 10 men who were joined on the way by three yeomen. The crown forces engaged the rebels at Ponsonby Bridge along the Grand Canal. Lieutenant Pearce wrote to his commanding officer at Rathcoole, Colonel Hunter, to inform him of the incident. Pearce alleged that his troop managed to kill 25 of the insurgents with only a hand wound from a pike being suffered by one of his sergeants.[39]

The following day, 21 June, Joseph Hewan, commanding a detachment of 20 Angushire Fencibles, was ordered to make his way from Tallaght to Hazelhatch in order to reinforce the garrison there.[40] The fencibles passed through Rathcoole on their march and stopped at the bakery in the village for sustenance. Soon after consuming the bread that the baker, Richard Fyans, had given them, the troops began to feel ill. One version of events found in the newspapers of the time stated that the symptoms displayed by the soldiers were those of a poisoning and that they were only saved due to the presence of the regimental surgeon.[41] Musgrave sought to set this episode against the backdrop of a renewed rebel effort to attack the village. He maintained that the rebels were 'indignant at the disappointment' at having their May offensive foiled and they planned to poison the garrison of the town while lying in wait in the surrounding countryside for the toxins to take effect. Musgrave's version of the episode lost credibility when he claimed that a Protestant clergyman, along with his seven children, also became poisoned when they ate the bread.[42] Pakenham has also dismissed this particular account as a fabrication and has placed it in the context of the multitude of fictitious atrocity stories that swept Dublin in mid-June 1798.[43] Fyans, the baker, and his apprentice, John Molloy, were taken into custody after the army surgeon Mr Irvine informed Colonel Hunter of what had happened. Doyle who 'kept a low publick house' was also suspected at first, but was later absolved.[44] The most logical explanation for the soldier's illness is that they had been drinking in Doyle's tavern and had left to raid Fyans' bakery but ended up either eating unbaked bread or simply eating too much and immediately felt unwell. Whether poison or alcohol caused the deterioration of the soldiers' health remains unclear but the suspected men, Richard Fyans and John Molloy, were taken up the village and shot near the church.[45] Michael Fyans, the great grandson of John Fyans the baker, recorded the episode in the 1940s as follows:

> The redcoats were out all night looking for rebels and early this morning they came into Rathcoole and they very hungry (sic). They raided the bakery and found a hot batch of bread just baked. Some of them took too much of the hot bread and buttermilk which was in the bakery and died. Mr. Fyans was accused of poisoning the food and he and an apprentice were taken out and shot in the Butheyes where the Garda Barrack is built.[46]

The village continued to remain unsettled towards the end of June and two days after the incident at Fyans two men entered Rathcoole and made what *Finn's Leinster Journal* described as 'menacing demands' of its inhabitants. The demands they made are unknown but the newspaper was clear that the pair were rebels who had been encamped in the neighbourhood of Rathcoole. According to the organ the 'messengers of treason received the due reward of treason in their immediate execution'.[47] Only two days passed again before the house of Thomas Brunton near the village was attacked by a number of insurgents on 25 June.[48]

In early July, the Clancys of Ballymount still feared their residence unsafe to live in. The family had moved to their city residence after the outbreak of rebellion. According to the head of the household, Patrick, they owed their safety in Dublin to the 'indefatigable zeal' of the city's yeomanry corps. Patrick sometimes returned to his country house to check on his remaining servants fearing they would abandon him if he did not.[49] Kelly has documented how rumours circulated among Protestants shortly after the outbreak of rebellion that its success in Dublin depended on servants turning against their masters.[50] This certainly influenced Patrick Clancy's decision to move to the city as it was apparent from the raid on their home in the months prior to the rising that there was truth to the rumours as some of the Clancy's servants had indeed turned against them, thus underlining the intimate nature of events. Moreover, that the Clancys had not returned to their home several weeks after all the main insurgent efforts had been suppressed, emphasized the danger which they perceived to still threaten that part of the county during the first weeks of July.

The Clancys were justified in their decision as rebel contingents continued to traverse the countryside throughout July. Undeterred by their final crushing losses in Wexford, and then at Carnew in Wicklow, a large detachment of rebels under the command of Fr Mogue Kearns made their way north to Whelp Rock. There they allied with Wicklow insurgents under General Joseph Holt. Also present at the camp were substantial numbers of Kildare rebels under Michael Murphy and Dublin city and county rebels under Colonel Edward Rattigan. A contingent under Colonel Felix Rourke had already joined the Wexford men at the battle of Hacketstown further south in Carlow.[51] In his book, *March into Meath*, Eamon Doyle has detailed how, on the advice of the Wexford priest Kearns, the rebels decided on marching through the midland counties in order to instigate a rising.[52] Felix Rourke was probably involved in this decision and in his own testimony described the insurgent strategy as having been to engage in a low-level guerrilla war and 'to march through the different counties in order to raise them, to avoid fighting as much as possible, but harass small parties'.[53] The United Irish contingent first set out for the rebel camp under Aylmer's charge at Timahoe, Co. Kildare. As they marched they passed the village of Prosperous, which by then had fallen back into the hands of the crown forces, and they were harried by soldiers as they skirted the village. Rourke later described the action near Prosperous to his sister Mary Finerty as follows:

> On perceiving a body of troops moving after us, we took up a strong position near the heights, above the town, a bog in front, only passable by a narrow road through which an army should march to attack … we had taken the precaution to place our bullocks, baggage &c., in such a situation on the road that our riflemen could fire with precision from behind us.[54]

Deterred by this manoeuvre, and by the numerous rebels who had taken up strong positions in the ditches, the troops drew back and the body of men under Rourke, and others such as Esmonde Kyan of Wexford, were able to continue unmolested so that they reached the insurgent camp at Timahoe under the command of Aylmer, Luby and Ware late in the evening of 10 July.[55]

Still reeling from the defeat at Ovidstown, Aylmer was in the middle of suing for terms of surrender through Lord Cornwallis and was less than enthused when the Whelp Rock contingent arrived at his camp. The following morning, without Aylmer and the majority of his men, the Whelp Rock rebels pushed northward to Clonard, Co. Meath. Upon reaching the outskirts of Clonard they mounted an attack in which Felix Rourke led the charge. According to Rourke they managed to make progress and they 'entered the town under a very warm fire of musquetry from the barracks'.[56] Felix Rourke's brother, Charles Rourke, was wounded during the course of the attempted advance on the village.[57] The rebel advance faltered when they came upon a well-manned and heavily fortified stone building that held a key strategic point in the village. The rebel band suffered heavy losses and were consequently forced to retreat. Rourke had already concocted a plan, following the unsuccessful attempt on Clonard, to return once again to the mountains in the hopes of restocking their supplies.[58] As they retreated back over the Kildare/Meath border the United Irish Army endured constant harassment by yeomen and by the Northumberland fencibles, eventually reaching Carbury where they camped for the night.[59] The following day, 12 July, they turned back towards Meath and took up a strong position on Knockderrig Hill, but they were caught by surprise by a combination of militia and dragoons under Lieutenant Colonel Gough. The insurgents had no choice but to retreat, leaving their provisions and baggage behind them. The constant harrying by government forces began to take its toll on the insurgents. Fatigue began to set in and groups of rebels dropped away from the main body as it headed further north to Slane. Rourke described a growing dissension among their ranks as the rebels of various counties 'separated ... and prejudiced the cause of liberty'.[60]

Not long afterwards, on 14 July, the contingent was finally disbanded when it reached Ballyboughill in north Co. Dublin. Under immense pressure from crown forces it was left to Esmonde Kyan to give the order to surrender their arms. Felix Rourke and his men had already left the main body of Wexford men and headed south-east for Whelp rock once more. Rourke was disappointed in the efforts to raise Kildare and upon reaching the western peripheries of the Wicklow mountains they were met, according to the Rathcoole man, by 'a horde of banditti ... formidable only to the unfortunate people'.[61] The men Rourke met there were not capable soldiers and there were only three captains remaining among the rebel contingent including Rourke himself. These circumstances, coupled with Lord Cornwallis having declared an amnesty for the rebels, prompted the decision by the rebel captains to send a flag of truce to Colonel Hunter at Rathcoole. Hunter granted Felix and Charles Rourke, Nicholas Lyons of Newcastle and Bartholomew Mahon a pass to meet with General Dundas. The men proceeded to Castlemartin House, headquarters of the British Army in Kildare, and on 7 August after meeting the general the Dublin city and county men finally surrendered.[62] The rebels received

protection for a number of days but were
then told that Dundas would no longer
grant them such without authority from
government and on 10 August they were
sent to gaol in Naas.[63] There they awaited
a decision from government that would
decide their future. Rourke wrote to
General Wilford, who had commanded
in Kildare during the rebellion, to
enquire about his and his comrades'
fate. In his reply Wilford stated that any
pardon which the men might receive
would be under the condition that they
would accept voluntary transportation.[64]
Rourke, however, was hopeful that
a number of people such as George
Ponsonby and the Revd Christopher
McAllister, clergyman of Rathcore in Meath, would assist in his seeking early
release from prison.[65]

6. Father James Harold

During the period of Rourke's confinement, Fr Harold (fig. 6), the local
Catholic priest at Rathcoole, was also apprehended and placed in prison. Dr
Troy, Catholic archbishop of Dublin, had appointed Harold as parish priest
of Kilcullen in 1789. In 1794, he was transferred to the parish of Saggart, of
which Rathcoole was a part. Harold had left Rathcoole at the outbreak
of rebellion. He preached two loyal sermons the Sunday before hostilities
commenced in which he called on his flock to 'shun all disorder and discord'.[66]
Yet, his condemnation of the local yeomanry's gratuitous use of violence and
his friendship with both Clinch and Rourke meant that he became suspected of
involvement with the Rathcoole United Irishmen and James Ormsby singled
out his house in Rathcoole for a weapons search. A military order was issued
for Harold's capture. He then fled as far south as Cork and back northwards
again to Drogheda, where he received written protection from the general in
command of that town.[67] Harold found his way back to Rathcoole during the
summer of 1798, where he stayed in hiding with a Protestant sympathizer and
friend at Hazelhatch. Harold came out of hiding after a time to say mass, but
on 18 August yeomen of the Rathcoole Cavalry seized him at the altar. Harold
showed the yeomen the writ of protection he had received but it was ignored
and he was brought under escort to Dublin.[68] *The Times* carried the story of the
clergyman's arrest, declaring that Harold had been 'accused by the unfortunate
Clinch at his dying moment as his seducer from his allegiance'.[69] Robert
Madden believed that it was a deliberate tactic of Orangemen in government
to pressurize rebels who had been found guilty of treason to denounce their
creed or to implicate the Catholic clergy in the rebellion before they were

put to death. Such seems to be the case with John Clinch who, according to Madden, 'uttered some unintelligible words, the name of Harold, and this was sufficient grounds for suspecting a priest of that name'.[70] Musgrave sought to implicate Harold as having sworn Clinch into the United Irishmen, stating that 'Clinch ... a humane and benevolent man was persuaded by the malignant influence of Fr Harold, his parish priest, to violate his oath of allegiance, and to become a traitor'.[71]

Despite his close association with both Clinch and Rourke it remains unclear if Harold was ever sworn in as a United Irishman. When Rourke, still imprisoned in early September, caught wind of the circumstances Harold was in, he strongly believed that the priest would be completely absolved. On 11 September, after receiving a request from the priest for assistance, Rourke described 'the futility of the charge under which [Harold] is confined in a military prison ... he is so conscious of his innocence, that he is quite certain if any man in power knew his situation, with the nature of the charges against him, that he would be liberated'.[72] On the other hand, Musgrave levelled the accusation against Harold that it was at his 'instigation ... the inhabitants of Rathcoole, and all the adjacent country, had swerved from their allegiance, and became traitors'. He went on to state that Harold wished to deceive the local magistracy by having the rebels surrender pikes, but specifically only ones that were in poor shape. The overtly sectarian tone throughout Musgrave's work, however, renders much of his evidence open to question.[73] It is possible that Harold denounced revolution only when Archbishop Troy issued a circular calling on the clergy to do so in the months leading up to the rebellion and that prior to that he had been a member of the secret society. However, evidence from Richard Sheil, who had known Harold personally for a long time and had many of the clergyman's stories recounted to him, would indicate that Harold never joined the United Irishmen. Sheil was convinced Harold had not joined and according to him the priest had told him 'that he knew no more of the rebellion or of United Irishmen or the crime that he was transported for than the child unborn. He was a first rate preacher and a good singer but knew nothing of worldly affairs'.[74] Ultimately, the evidence to hand points towards Harold not having been involved in radical activities.

Towards the end of August Rourke's efforts in drumming up support from his cell in Naas gaol began to be rewarded. On 21 August, the Revd McAllister wrote to Edward Kennedy, magistrate at Rathcoole, in an effort to have Rourke and his comrades released. Rourke and Nicholas Lyons, who served as a captain under him, were mentioned favourably by McAllister in his correspondence. Both had passed by the clergyman's house at Summerhill in Meath on 12 July while on their ill-fated march northwards. While the rebels were at his home, and again demonstrating the personal nature of the conflict, McAllister was accused of being an Orangeman by one of his servants, whom he described as 'a wretch who had eaten his bread for years'.[75] Rebels present from Wexford, where sectarianism and reprisal killings had been a feature, brandished their guns and threatened to kill the clergyman and his family. Around 40 Wexford rebels prepared to set fire to McAllister's house when Rourke and Lyons intervened to save the property and the family's lives, according to the clergyman, 'at the hazard of their own'.[76]

McAllister's plea to Kennedy was unsuccessful as Rourke and his comrades were still confined in Naas at the end of August. By 30 August, Rourke had gotten word of the French landing at Killala, where a force of some 1,100 men had landed on the Mayo coast under the command of General Jean Humbert. Rourke's attitude to the French landing was one of bitterness at first as he believed that the French presence worsened his own predicament as the government utilized the situation to keep Rourke and his comrades imprisoned while the invasion force continued to pose a threat. Initially, he was pessimistic about the chances of any French success, stating that they had only come 'to inspire the rebels with fresh hopes, and again to disappoint them, *à la Bantry*'.[77] After receiving word of the French and United Irish victory at Castlebar, however, Rourke's attitude changed to one of regret at not having been able to join up with the invasion force. Knowing what he did now, that the French had landed, Rourke began to see his own surrender as a mistake. Had he still been free he would have brought his men to fight at the battle of Ballinamuck on 8 September, where the French were defeated by General Lake and the end of open rebellion in 1798 was marked.[78]

By early autumn Rathcoole had returned to a state of tranquillity. Rourke remained confined despite the efforts of Peter Locke, a member of the local minor gentry, to convince General Dundas of his good character.[79] Meanwhile, the Clancys, feeling it safe to venture from their city residence, had returned to Ballymount where William, demonstrating the effect of the rebellion in moving moderate Protestants to actively maintain their social positions as pro-government loyalists, immersed himself in studying military tactics.[80] It was not until mid-November that an act of political violence occurred again in the neighbourhood. Several miles from the village the house of a Mr Phillips was raided and afterwards burned by rebels. His son who had been in the Rathcoole cavalry was also reported missing for a time until his body turned up in the mountains south-west of Rathcoole at Kilteel.[81] He had been lured into the mountains by three or four rebels where he was killed and his body half-buried. Musgrave sought to attribute a sectarian motive to the assassination, stating that 'a party of ruffians … declared, that their vengeance was occasioned by [Phillips' son] being a protestant and in the yeomen'.[82] As already noted, Musgrave's testimony ought to be viewed critically. If indeed he is correct in his assertion that Phillips' religion was a motivating factor then this incident stands as the only recorded instance of sectarian violence in the area. It was, in fact, more likely that Phillips had been targeted because he was a loyalist and part of the yeomanry corps who had played a significant part in thwarting the rebellion locally. Kevin O'Neill has pointed out how the prominent Quaker diarist of the rebellion, Mary Leadbeater, has placed the actions of the rebels in the aftermath of defeat in south Kildare in context. According to O'Neill, rather than blunt sectarianism, Leadbeater 'offers other explanatory variables that locate the source of violence in revenge for economic exploitation, traditional land disputes, and the pressure of impossible circumstances faced by the defeated rebels'.[83]

Towards the end of November 1798 Patrick Clancy wrote to his son James and laid bare his feelings on Wolfe Tone. Tone had recently been captured attempting to land a French fleet at Lough Swilly and was to be court-martialled and hanged. After Tone cut his own throat to avoid hanging, Clancy, displaying an acute personal enmity towards the United Irish leader, stated:

> I think with respect to Mr Tone, that he might as well be hanged by the sentence of martial as common law, for death he certainly deserves, for he was deeply implicated [in the rebellion], & notwithstanding govt. generously suffered him to escape, I gave a large sum of money to take himself and family to America, so that for this act of ingratitude, if nothing else, he deserves punishment.[84]

As 1798 came to a close a number of government supporters from the area lodged requests for compensation with Dublin Castle. John Mullan of Rathcoole requested the sum of £174 3s. 11d. for the loss of his house and offices which had stood in the centre of the village and had been set ablaze by the rebels. From nearby Saggart, William Smyth had lost a number of horses and sought £20 compensation. The most telling requests came, however, from residents of Brittas, a small townland to the south of Rathcoole just over the hills which rise above the village. William Goucher sought the substantial sum of £430 1s. 6d. for the loss of his house and cattle. Similar applications were lodged by John, Henry and Thomas O'Brien, who between them requested compensation of nearly £700 from government. They had lost a house, rent, furniture, as well as food stocks of oatmeal, potatoes, and cattle.[85] The losses incurred on these wealthy farmers was indicative of strong rebel activity during the course of the year in the high ground that rises above Rathcoole. Bands of insurgents roamed the hills stocking up on food and fuel while awaiting the opportunity to descend on the strategic village and its garrison. This opportunity never came for the United Irishmen in 1798. Yet, this did not mean that the rebels in the area had become demoralized to the point that they abandoned their convictions. Radical thought endured among the lower classes in politicized areas such as Rathcoole for a number of years and would eventually culminate in a second attempt at rebellion in Dublin.

3. Aftermath, 1799–1803

This chapter examines the fallout from the 1798 rebellion. Between the years 1799 and 1803 efforts to free imprisoned rebels, continued disaffection and violence, heightened suspicion of those thought to be engaging in seditious behaviour, and a second attempted rising all impacted on Rathcoole and its inhabitants to varying degrees. With John Clinch having been executed following the rising, Felix Rourke and his brothers remained as Rathcoole's chief United Irishmen.

In the opening months of 1799 some of Rathcoole's local power brokers began a concerted campaign to have the Rourke brothers released after they had spent Christmas confined to their cells in Naas. Central to this effort were magistrates and landowners, among them Edward Kennedy of Johnstown House and Alexander Graydon. Peter Locke, who had already assisted in gaining the release of a number of other local rebels, also played a key role. Locke was a Catholic who would later make a large financial contribution to the construction of a chapel at Newcastle.[1] He may well have been friends with the Rourkes, who were in turn close acquaintances of Fr Harold's. Therefore, Locke's support for the Catholic Church in the locality and his common religious ground with the Rourkes may have influenced his decision to assist them.[2] In his petitions to government Locke maintained he had substantial knowledge of the Rourkes' conduct during the course of the rebellion and that it had been humane throughout, while he also pointed out that the brothers had not been implicated in any atrocities as others had been throughout the violent summer. Locke was certain that he would not be promoting their release if he thought it endangered the peace in Rathcoole.[3] He argued that to free the men could be seen as a move against his own interests if he was not fully sure they would leave Rathcoole undisturbed as his 'whole property is situated there or very near to it'. Had the Rourkes once again engaged in rebellious action the repercussions for Locke would be serious. Locke therefore urged Kennedy and Graydon, along with Thomas Brunlow and William Brunton, to add their names to the petitions and suggested that other minor gentry figures in the neighbourhood were also supportive. According to Locke the pardoning of local rebels prior to this had ensured revenge attacks on loyalists had not been a major issue in Rathcoole and he claimed that in the way of such reprisals the 'district suffered nothing during the rebellion or since'.[4] Although Locke's claim was an exaggerated one and many petitions glossed over the facts to have the desired effect on their reader, there was some truth in his statement as Rathcoole avoided serious post-rebellion violence such as that which had materialized most forcefully to the south in the Wicklow mountains under the leadership of Michael Dwyer.[5]

From behind bars Felix Rourke waged his own campaign to free himself. He managed to convince an army captain by the name of Owens to petition on his behalf. In July Owens had been taken prisoner by those under Rourke's command during their march through Kildare and Meath. Following the unsuccessful attempt on Clonard while the rebels were falling back to Carbury, Captain Owens was taken into the personal custody of Rourke. The 'sanguinary disposition' of the Wexford rebels was triggered when they noticed Owens was wearing an orange ribband around his arm. Rourke protected Owens from the Wexford men's intentions and took the army captain as far as Nineteen-mile Bridge where they parted company. In January 1799, Rourke then wrote to Owens seeking the favour be returned to him. Owens obliged and sent a letter addressed to Alexander Marsden, a government official in Dublin Castle, requesting that Rourke be shown leniency as he was 'highly indebted' to the Rathcoole man for his personal safety. Despite the efforts of Owens and Locke, on 21 January a Castle bureaucrat, Lieutenant Colonel Littlehales, re-assessed the Rourkes brothers' case and denied their plea. Littlehales stated that he had made 'further inquiry as to the character of these men and I have every reason to think them unfit for being released'.[6] Rourke suspected that foul play on the part of Charles Ormsby was behind his continued confinement. 'But for the machinations of the villain ... I would now be at liberty; but ... his baneful influence blights all the fair hopes I entertained'.[7]

While the Rourkes remained imprisoned, those rebels who had avoided capture and execution continued to live as fugitives. Liam Chambers has stated that, with the exception of Dwyer in Wicklow, no major figures emerged to harness the leaderless United Irishmen during this period and that, as a result, 'rebellion and robbery overlapped'.[8] Patterson has emphasized the continued politicization of the lower classes in the years immediately following the 1798 rebellion. He notes the persistence of state-sponsored violence and repression as a catalyst for 'pervasive popular alienation' and the possibility of a renewed revolt by United Irishmen in 1803. Emmet's rising, he argues, was also the result of long term trends through the 1790s, a decade in which middle class radicals had succeeded in propagating their United Irish doctrine.[9] Locally, reports of attacks and robberies continued to be made. In contradiction to Locke's statement about reprisals not having been a problem, in January 1799 a number of armed rebels attacked the house of Mr Egan near Tallaght and killed his yeoman son.[10] Violent robberies, which at times appeared to take place out of desperation to attain supplies, were also carried out by fugitive rebels who refused to surrender. At the end of February a grocer and a dairy man were robbed and killed at Tallaght Hill and a publican in Ballyfermot was killed while attempting to defend his house against a band of raiders. *The Times* reported on the attacks in the area, stating that 'outrages of a very atrocious nature still continue'.[11]

By March 1799, the continuing threat the rebels still posed in Rathcoole was substantiated by the fact that government ordered two companies of militia under Majors Sirr and Swan, accompanied by the yeomanry cavalry, to scour the flatlands from Crumlin out to Tallaght. Their orders were to afterwards proceed towards the Wicklow mountains. The yeomen who rode out towards the mountains were reported by the *Freeman's Journal* to have seen in a number of places 'at a distance, insurgents making off at their approach' while they searched 'some wretched cabins and huts ... as they went along and found them well stocked with oats and oatmeal'.[12] The impressive quantity of provisions accumulated by the mountain-based rebels indicated that they intended to hold out and conduct guerrilla warfare in expectation of another rising. But as the year 1799 wore on attacks in the area became less frequent. The insurgents most likely began to return home as the possibility of a renewed attempt faded and the hardship of their lives on the run started to wear them down.

Fr Harold, who had been taken prisoner in August 1798, still remained incarcerated at the beginning of 1799. He had been kept on board a vessel named the *Lively* in Dublin bay since the previous November but was transferred to the *Minerva* in Cork harbour in the spring of 1799 in lieu of transportation to Australia. Two men known only by their surnames, Ryan and Lamb, both from Dublin city and friends of the clergyman, drew up a petition on Harold's behalf on 28 February and addressed it to Lord Castlereagh. In it they urged the chief secretary to consider the priest's position as he was 55 at the time and 'under a variety of infirmities which he could not long endure'. Ryan and Lamb requested that Harold be freed in order to stand trial, so confident were they that he would be exonerated from having been involved in the rebellion. According to the petitioners Harold could 'shew by incontestable proof that instead of countenancing the late unhappy rebellion he has used every power in his means to suppress it'.[13] Castlereagh agreed with the content of the petition and issued a writ of habeas corpus in the priest's favour. Lamb and Ryan went to the dock where the *Minerva* was anchored to issue the notice to have Harold brought off the prison ship but the captain would not let them on board to serve the notice. John Rourke, another of Felix Rourke's brothers, swore a pledge in front of a judge and a second order to have Harold freed was issued, but that also met with the same outcome.[14] Fr James Harold was transported on the convict ship *Minerva* in the summer of 1799 and arrived in Sydney, Australia, on 11 January 1800. Upon his arrival in Australia, Father Harold found himself in the thick of a rebel plot once again. The rebels who had been transported after the rising sought to stage a revolt in the new colony. Harold divulged the plot to the Sydney authorities and was afterwards called to give evidence against the conspirators, which he duly did – a fact that bolsters the assertion that Harold had no part in United Irish activity in Rathcoole.[15] After

a period in the United States, following his time in Australia, Harold returned
to Ireland in 1815. He served again in his old parish of Kilcullen and then in
Fairview/Clontarf. He died in 1830 aged 85 and is buried in Goldenbridge
Cemetery in Dublin.[16]

By March 1799 the four Co. Dublin rebels in Naas gaol – Felix and Bryan
Rourke, Bartholomew Mahon and Nicholas Lyons – determined on appealing
by petition to a higher authority, namely Lord Lieutenant Cornwallis. It
appears, however, that Charles Ormsby's influence hindered their efforts once
again. Ormsby was not acquainted with Mahon or Lyons, but in his countering
letter to the petition he was vitriolic in his condemnation of the Rourkes. He
had, understandably, taken it as a personal insult that Felix Rourke had taken
part in the plot to conspire to kill him and overthrow his corps of yeomen
and he described the brothers as 'two of the most ungrateful and unprincipled
rebels in the country'. Ormsby maintained that the Rourkes had engaged in
'nefarious underhand practices', which had put him in unnecessary danger while
the rebellion was raging by forcing him to disarm his yeomen and deal with
them accordingly. In June 1799, Ormsby, writing from his residence in Dawson
Street, again obstructed the efforts of the Rourke brothers to be released. 'The
astonishing art of these fellows, their apparent loyalty as yeomen at the very
time they were organizing the whole country round them makes them appear to
me as far indeed from the Lord Lieutenant's favour'. Referring to John Clinch,
Ormsby stated that Rourke's 'lieutenant was executed at Newgate for half their
crimes'.[17] By the close of 1799 Felix Rourke had lost any hint of optimism and
several months later in 1800, his spirits at their lowest ebb, he was led to state
'how true the adage is, "that hope deferred, maketh the heart sick" … the old
story of tomorrow is kept up, till credulity sickened, can believe no more'.[18]

During Rourke's captivity throughout 1799 and the first half of 1800 outside
of the prison walls a debate raged on the introduction of the act of Union.
Although calls had been made for a union as early as 1797, the rebellion provided
the necessary context for its imposition. Rourke, in fact, supported the move as
he viewed it as the only measure capable of protecting the people 'from a vile
aristocracy that would reduce the government of the country to a corporation,
and create a system of robbing, under the patronage of an ascendancy club'.[19]
However, Madden afterwards remarked that Rourke's support for the Union
must be viewed in light of the litany of coercive measures directed at the United
Irishmen which had been introduced by the Irish parliament.[20] Patrick Clancy
of Ballymount provided his own interpretation of public opinion with regard
to a union in late 1798. 'Should such an event take place, the generality of our
countrymen, the aristocracy in particular will be highly displeased, indeed some
say it will ultimately produce a separation'.[21] In December he wrote:

> New ballads [against the union] assail us at every printers, & new
> emblematical ribbands with 'no union, freedom & independence to

Ireland', they are all bought with avidity ... all ranks are crying out against the measure, & as for my own part, I wish it were carried quietly, as I fear the consequences of pressing it.[22]

When the debate on the act of Union ended two acts were passed simultaneously in the British and Irish houses of commons to establish a union during the summer of 1800.[23] Although the debate on the act had been fierce inside the Irish house of commons, the divisiveness remained a feature of high-politics and did not instigate violence in the countryside. Rathcoole remained quiet during the period 1800–2. The only two reports during these years concerning military or criminal activities were relatively minor. The *Albion and Evening Advertiser* reported in June that the 24th Light Dragoons were to be stationed in Rathcoole for the remainder of 1800.[24] In February 1801 the *Freeman's Journal* reported on the theft of two bullocks from a Mr Buckley, probably a relative of the assassinated landowner.[25] The purchase of a substantial amount of lands in Rathcoole by David Latouche in 1801 reflected the tranquillity the area experienced. After the turbulent years of the rebellion had passed, Latouche considered it a prudent time to invest and bought the majority of James Ormsby's lands in Rathcoole for the sum of £12,000.[26] However, the extended period of peace was in many ways superficial as political organization in the wider area did not suddenly cease. Chambers' study of Co. Kildare has illustrated that 'the crucial point about the period 1798 to 1802 is that political radicalism continued to persist among the lower orders'.[27] Groups such as those led by Michael Doorly, who held out in the inaccessible areas of Kildare, continued to espouse United Irish sentiment.[28]

In Rathcoole, one instance that came to the attention of government during this period was the case of the magistrate for Newcastle, Captain Alexander Graydon. A minor gentry figure, Graydon lived at Newcastle House.[29] He had petitioned for the release of the Rourkes on a number of occasions throughout 1799 and early 1800 but had met with no success.[30] Graydon was driven to what government deemed seditious activities during 1800. He may have seen the refusal of his pleas to have the Rourke brothers released as an affront to his status or it may have been that he simply became angered with the inaction on the part of the government over the two-year period. Whatever his motives Graydon was informed upon by Private Laen, who passed correspondence to Alexander Marsden in the Castle in which he stated that Graydon had been 'expressing himself in a treasonable manner'.[31] On 24 February an anonymous informant sent a letter to government concerning the Newcastle magistrate. The information stated that Graydon had gone to the chapel at Newcastle the previous Sunday to attempt to raise the congregation to take up arms. After the churchgoers told him they could do nothing as they had no weapons, Graydon assured them that he would supply them with such and any other provisions they required. Graydon then allegedly stated that 'he was not afraid of all the militia kept in Ireland'.[32] It is likely that Graydon reacted emotionally after having received word that another petition of his had been rejected. Had he been serious about a conspiracy and gathering arms rational thought would have told him that there were better ways to go about it than announcing his intentions during Sunday Mass. It appears that Graydon may have been threatened by government or imprisoned for a period as there is no indication of increased organization in the area. On the surface the Castle may have had little to be concerned about when it came to United Irish activity during the opening two to three years of the 19th century in the Rathcoole neighbourhood, but the statements of the Mass goers that they could not act as they had no arms is indicative of a simmering disaffection, albeit without the necessary leadership.

That leadership would soon re-emerge when Felix Rourke eventually took up his role as a United Irish figurehead once more. Rourke had been released in the summer of 1800 and he afterwards made his way to Ulster where he found himself in poor circumstances, earning a meagre wage from a career on the stage as a comic character in Belfast. In 1801, he returned to Dublin and took up a post as a clerk in a brewery owned by a Mr Robinson near St Stephen's Green.[33] Soon after his return to the capital he once again became politically active and established contact with his close friend, Bartholomew Mahon, whom he had known prior to the rebellion and spent time with in Naas gaol.[34] Robert Emmet, who had taken part in the 1798 rebellion but left for France in its wake, returned to Ireland in late 1802 and soon set about organizing a conspiracy which sought to attack the administration at its heart in Dublin. As leader of the rejuvenated United Irish networks Emmet began to establish numerous arms factories throughout the city where the manufacture of gunpowder, pikes, rockets and other arms took place.[35] Rourke was centrally involved in Emmet's developing plans for a rising and he hoped to convince Mahon to take part in the forthcoming rebellion. As plans progressed, Rourke had held a meeting with the remaining Wicklow and Kildare United Irish leaders in an effort to co-ordinate their march on Dublin upon the outbreak of this second rebellion.[36]

The abovementioned case of Captain Graydon in 1800 appears, on the surface, to have been the only call to arms or hint of conspiratorial organization in the Rathcoole area in the aftermath of the 1798 rebellion, but preparations for Emmet's rising in the neighbourhood had been underway since early 1803. On the morning of the intended rebellion on 23 July Emmet dispatched emissaries who rode out to Athgoe, Hazelhatch and Rathcoole to alert established contacts in the area that the rising was to occur that evening.[37] Government appears to have been unaware of this organization as the constant instances of house raids that had occurred before the outbreak of rebellion five years earlier did not occur this time round. Emmet's Dublin focussed strategy and use of secret arms depots rather than locally based United Irish offensives, as occurred in Rathcoole during 1798, also made it less likely the administration would detect activity outside of the capital.

On the day of the planned rebellion, Charles Rourke, owner of a tavern in Thomas Street and brother to Felix, allowed men to gather in his establishment where, according to Madden, 'there were crowds of country people drinking and smoking, in the highest spirits, cracking jokes, and rallying one another, as if the business they were about to enter on was a party of pleasure'.[38]

Felix Rourke was hurriedly passing back and forth between the tavern and John Hevey's house at 41 Thomas Court where some of the leaders were gathered.[39] Although Felix Rourke was appointed to command a body of Co. Dublin rebels that were to assemble at the Coombe, the slipshod nature of the rising meant that this never came to pass. Due to an unfortunate explosion that had occurred at a rocket depot on Patrick Street on 16 July, Emmet's hand was forced and the attempt was wrought with poor coordination and confused reports from the outset. The planned rebellion and attack on the Castle descended into a hasty march up Thomas Street on 23 July that ended abruptly when Emmet issued countermanding orders upon the realization that any hopes of success had evaporated.[40]

Much as in 1798 rebels had planned to march in from Dublin's suburbs and Kildare to meet the city men. Bartholomew Mahon did in fact manage to make his way into Dublin with a body of men from Naas on 23 July. However, as plans went awry Mahon and his band of Kildare rebels failed to link up with Emmet and the city men at the market house on Thomas Street as had been intended.[41] Activity in Rathcoole on 23 July was limited to the movements of local and country insurgents towards the capital. Laurence Dillon, deputy postmaster of Rathcoole, wrote to the Castle authorities the next day. He informed under-secretary Edward Cooke that the parish and town of Rathcoole were in a state of 'great fermentation'. Dillon was unaware as to the cause of this ferment, but was unknowingly alluding to the upsurge of underground activity in the hours before the rising.[42]

Despite the lack of any violent actions in the Rathcoole neighbourhood on 23 July, the most prominent casualty of Emmet's rising lived in the Rathcoole area. Arthur Wolfe held the title of Lord Kilwarden and the post of chief justice of the king's bench in Ireland. He resided at Newlands, just over three miles from Rathcoole.[43] Colonel Finlay had left the city under cavalry escort when he realized that the threat from the rebels posed a considerable danger and he informed Kilwarden of this when he reached his home in Corkagh near Newlands. Kilwarden ignored the warning and made his way into Dublin due to a miscalculation on his own part that he would be safer in the city than he would have been in his country residence.[44] When the carriage he was travelling in made its way toward Dublin Castle it was stopped at the centre of the rising's activity on Thomas Street. A throng of rebels proceeded to take Lord Kilwarden and his nephew, the Revd Richard Wolfe, from the coach and pike them to death. The incident unnerved the establishment and large rewards were offered for any information about the deaths.[45] Bryan Rourke was suspected of having been involved in Kilwarden's demise. This suspicion was fuelled by his relationship to Felix Rourke, but also because he had been wounded on the same day fighting in the city.[46]

The *Freeman's Journal* reported one instance of violence in the Rathcoole neighbourhood in the period surrounding Emmet's rising, which came about as a result of the imagined threat the rising caused rather than by any coordinated United Irish effort. A group of yeomen from the Rathcoole area had gone to Dublin to patrol on 24 July after receiving word of the rising. Among them was Mr Booth, a farmer from Newcastle, as well as the Revd Jones and Richard Jones of Rathcoole.[47] On their way out of the city they stopped by Colonel Finlay's house at Corkagh Demesne near Clondalkin and he advised them to stay the night at his house for their own safety. On the morning of 25 July they rose at an early hour and intended to complete the short journey to Rathcoole. They passed by the gunpowder mills in Clondalkin and as they were out of uniform the guards on duty, conscious of the strategic importance of the mills they were defending and aware of events in the city, fired upon the yeomen. Booth was killed instantly, as was the horse on which the clergyman Jones rode, while Richard Jones was severely wounded.[48]

In the wake of the 1803 rising Bartholomew Mahon, Felix Rourke and his youngest brother, Matthew, left the city and made their way to Mahon's house where they stayed for several days. For reasons not quite clear, and despite the efforts of Mahon to convince him otherwise, Felix Rourke returned to the city sometime in August. Shortly after he arrived in Dublin, Rourke was spotted by Alderman Bloxham as he watched government troops drill outside their barracks in the Coombe, and he was subsequently arrested. Madden commented that Rourke 'appeared to have entertained no fear of being arrested'. The Rathcoole rebel seems to have been resigned to defeat after the failure of the second rising in which he had taken part. Rourke was supposed to have commanded a large body of rebels and marched on the city on the night of 23 July from the Coombe and he may well have returned there in August to ponder what might have been. After having been taken into custody by Bloxham, Rourke stood trial for high treason in Dublin on 6 September 1803.[49]

Felix Rourke was accused, along with John Killen and John Mac Cann, of killing a watchman and a dragoon while calling on his men to do their duty and free Ireland. The prosecution's main witness was Michael Mahaffy who described seeing Rourke on Bridgefoot Street on the night in question dressed in a white riding coat with a dark green coat with plated buttons underneath. George Ponsonby, one of Rourke's counsels for defence, was adamant that Mahaffy was actually with the rebels but had fled once plans went awry and only later testified against them in an effort to cover himself. Mahaffy denied this and claimed that he had been in the vicinity of the rising and fled out of fear. He had made his way down Meath Street with John Ryan, who also testified, and then on to Tallaght Hill. From there Mahaffy and Ryan travelled to Mountrath in Queen's Co. where they were taken in by a local magistrate. Mahaffy immediately divulged all he had allegedly seen around Thomas Street. His credibility was damaged when he claimed he had taken no part in the rebellion, yet he had fled a distance of nearly 50 miles, allegedly out of fear, after the rising had failed.[50]

John Philpot Curran, also defending Rourke, called Mahaffy's character and honesty into question and pointed out the numerous inconsistencies in the several accounts he had given. Curran cross examined Mahaffy and brought to light that he had been accused of being a conman, had broken an oath of temperance and was disliked by the majority of the corps of his Kildare militia who had alienated him for 'abusing persons of the common and ordinary rank of life'.[51] A number of other witnesses also provided an alibi for Rourke, including his brother Matthew, who stated that he was in his brother John's tavern, the Golden Bottle or the Yellow Bottle, at the time of his alleged involvement and that he was not wearing clothes anything like those Mahaffy had described.[52] Madden stated that Rourke's comrades who were with him that night denounced Mahaffy's evidence as 'a tissue of fabrications'.[53] After hearing from one of the judges on what they ought to consider, the jury retired to deliberate. Whatever Rourke's exact movements on the evening of 23 July his central involvement in the 1798 Rebellion and his having escaped without transportation or execution would have influenced the jurors. Whether or not Rourke committed the specific acts levelled against him would have been a secondary issue in the minds of the jury to his involvement in rebellion for a second time, and after only ten minutes they returned with a verdict of guilty. Upon the announcement of the verdict Rourke addressed the court. 'My lord, I am conscious that I am not guilty of all the crimes imputed to me, and therefore my fortitude does not forsake me. I appeal to that God, before whose throne I must shortly appear, that I am innocent of the facts sworn to by the witnesses.'[54] Rourke's pleas fell on deaf ears and having been found guilty of high treason he was sentenced to be executed outside his father's door in Broadfield, Rathcoole. Four days later on 10 September Rourke, with a substantial escort of yeomen, was brought from Newgate prison where he had been held to his native village to be hanged. The *Freeman's Journal* reported the scene as he left the prison:

> Rourke ... endeavoured to affect fortitude, and to battle a shivering he was seized with, being asked was he easy in his mind he said he was perfectly composed; he went in a smart pace from the gaol into the cart and sat on the side going to the gallows ... and as he went from the prison bowed his head to those he saw in the windows, signifying farewell to his former comrades; on his way he looked much about in the town; instead of paying attention to his book.[55]

When Rourke reached Rathcoole he was met by Captain Bernard Clynch, a magistrate from Peamount near Newcastle, whom Madden later described as 'one of the terrorists of his day'.[56] Clynch, although spelling his surname slightly differently, was likely related in some way to the Clinches of Rathcoole. In 1804, he would capture one of the last remaining high-ranking rebels in the Wicklow mountains, John Mernagh. *The Times* reported that Clynch apprehended Mernagh and four rebels who 'had no firearms but pelted the military with stones'.[57] The Rourkes were spared the added grief of having their son executed outside their home as the influence of a local gentleman and family friend – quite possibly Peter Locke – saw that part of the sentence dismissed. Instead, Rourke was brought to the burnt-out house of Fr Harold where Clynch made every effort through the use of gratuitous violence to solicit a reaction from him and endeavoured to deny the attending priest administer the last rites to the condemned man. Rourke remained calm and dignified. He was hanged from one of the rafters of Harold's former home. *Johnson's British Gazette*, as well as the *Freeman's Journal*, reported that during the execution the village of Rathcoole appeared to be deserted of its inhabitants and that not a single person wearing colourful clothing was seen.[58] Rourke's body was handed over to his friends who had him buried at a site known as Bully's Acre, on the grounds of the Royal Hospital in Kilmainham where Robert Emmet was also later interred.[59] Like Clynch, Rourke's final letter was lacking in defiance, but instead, perhaps with his relatives in mind, pled innocence:

> Newgate Prison
>
> 9 September 1803
>
> Dear honoured father and mother
>
> For the last time I address you in this world hoping to convey to your minds that peace and consolation I feel and which I trust will support you in that moment which tomorrow is destined to terminate my life. My innocence inspires me with a fervent hope of meeting through the merits of a crucified Jesus that mercy which He promised all who would truly repent and avail themselves of the opportunity held out by His suffering.
>
> I remain dear Sir and Madam
>
> With love to brothers and sister
>
> Your dutiful and I hope happy Son
>
> Felix Rourke.[60]

Rourke's co-accused John Mac Cann and John Killen were executed several days later in Thomas Street.[61] The Kildare rebel Bernard Duggan stated years later to Madden that of the 20 people the government put to death following Emmet's rising 'there were only four men who were really concerned in the conspiracy, namely – Mr Emmet, Henry Howley, Felix Rourke, and Mr Russell'.[62] The Rathcoole man had evidently played a key role in planning the rising, yet his native village had not come under the scope of those plans and it had remained largely unaffected by the political turmoil of 1803.

A number of Rathcoole locals nevertheless found themselves on the receiving end of government repression in the wake of Emmet's attempt. The administration's obvious unease at a repeat of the 1798 rebellion saw it imprison anyone suspected of subversive behaviour after the 1803 rising. Notwithstanding his rank as a captain in the Rathcoole Cavalry, and his social status as a prominent figure of the locality's minor gentry, Edward Kennedy was imprisoned for 'treasonable practices' in 1804.[63] Another of Felix Rourke's brothers, John Rourke, was also held in custody in Kilmainham gaol for 'treasonable practices' from December of 1803 until the summer of 1804. His brother Bryan was arrested in the summer of 1804 on the same grounds and was still in confinement in 1805.[64] Both Bryan Rourke and Edward Kennedy took a libel action against the *Freeman's Journal* for accusing them in its edition of 26 May 1804 of disorderly conduct while they were gaoled.[65] John Rourke had lost what little land he had following 1798 and ended up living in dire poverty in the Liberties with a large family, having emerged from his time in gaol a broken man.[66] Like Alexander Graydon before him it is likely that Edward Kennedy's earlier support for the Rourkes and his petitioning on their behalf singled him out for scrutiny by those in Rathcoole who showed less leniency towards the rebels. Whatever the reasons behind Kennedy having been taken to Kilmainham gaol, or Graydon having been informed upon, loyalists in the neighbourhood who had foiled the rising in 1798 consolidated their positions again after 1803 and remained on high alert thereafter, suspecting even those who had assisted in suppressing the rising only five years previously.

Conclusion

Although the absence of accounts, memoirs, and letters by Rathcoole's lower-class inhabitants in an age which predated widespread literacy and personal written communication makes it difficult to discern precise motivations, some conclusions about their rationale for action can nevertheless be drawn. Sectarianism was not a major motivating factor in the recruitment of locals to the United Irish cause, nor was it central to how the rebellion unfolded in Rathcoole. Such a conclusion might jar somewhat with those elements in the historical profession who, in the last decade or more, have been attempting to portray more recent phases of republican insurrection as having been driven by religious hatred. In Rathcoole, sectarian attitudes and resentments had certainly been present in the village during the late 18th century, but that both Mercer's School and the Church of Ireland church survived the years of rebellion, unlike landmarks of the Protestant faith elsewhere, was significant. That tolerance was the order of the day in Rathcoole is unsurprising when the anti-sectarian, republican credentials of the village's chief United Irish organizer, Felix Rourke, are taken into account. The campaign by Rathcoole's liberal minor-gentry figures in the wake of the 1798 rebellion to free imprisoned rebels certainly contributed to decreasing the likelihood of retaliatory sectarian attacks in the post-rebellion phase. Ormsby and his loyalist associates had, nonetheless, acted as a tool of suppression by keeping the rebellion down. Their actions were not quickly forgotten by Rathcoole's United Irishmen and two local yeomen met their demise in revenge for their part in foiling rebel plans. Yet, no sectarian motive could be attributed to these assassinations.

Rather than emanating from within the rebel camp, as the historiographical narrative has sometimes asserted of events in Wexford for instance, sectarianism in Rathcoole derived from the establishment. It was Ormsby who introduced sectarianism and ultra-Protestant distrust of the conspiratorial 'papist' into the equation when he suspected the evidently non-revolutionary cleric, Fr Harold, of United Irish involvement. Likewise, it was the administration who employed a sectarian policy of coercing captured rebels into implicating Catholic priests, as occurred in the case of John Clinch and Fr Harold. Later, Musgrave also determined on proving Harold's complicity in the rebel plot and portraying the politically motivated revenge killing of the yeoman at Kilteel as part of a plan to exterminate Protestants. As Kelly has noted, the recollection of 'atrocity stories' by Protestants and the perseverance of myths in the years that followed 1798 took primacy over actual events in the formation of their attitudes.[1]

Nineteenth-century Irish politics and society – often split along denominational lines – proved how Musgrave's narrative soon became the prevailing one among many Protestants while, unfortunately, the efforts of figures such as Rourke to combat the corrosive presence of religious intolerance were all but forgotten.

Despite sectarian animosity not having been prevalent in Rathcoole between the years 1797–1803, political and social polarization was still a marked feature in the area. The wealthier farmers came to be pitted against the mostly lower-class rebels who attacked their homesteads throughout the course of 1797 and 1798. Rourke and Ormsby embodied the broader ideological clash between radical and conservative in the locality. Rourke had been a member of the small farming class and a yeoman under Ormsby's command. At some point during the 1790s, United Irish influences saw him move into the radical camp and turn against the yeomen, thus demonstrating on an individual level how former colleagues became politically polarized from one another. Meanwhile, the change in opinion of those in the Clancy household from moderate to reactionary was indicative of how the experience of traumatic one-off events – in this case, a violent house raid – could push different actors into polarized camps.

Ultimately, British colonialism, which the United Irishmen sought to break with, provided the context for sectarian and political polarization. Through a process of mass politicization and propagandizing, republicans created the specific conditions for an attack on the status quo. Rathcoole's scattered landholding patterns mitigated against the emergence of Defender networks and highly influential landlords or mercantile figures that had laid the basis for mobilization elsewhere from the mid-1790s. It was left to United Irish agents to politicize the local populace, an endeavour that was duly undertaken and began to bear fruit when house attacks with military objectives increased steadily through 1797. The existence of a levelling philosophy, which operated in tandem with political objectives, was detectable in these house raids and in the 1798 rebellion which followed. Prior to the spread of United Irish ideology in the predominantly rural community of Rathcoole, agrarian violence had not manifested in the area in any significant way. Relations between landlord and tenant, like those between farmer and labourer, were not strained to breaking point as they were in other districts. Yet, the emerging agrarian capitalist social structure of Rathcoole, which bestowed advantage on the middle and upper classes and consigned a majority to toil in the fields, bred a deep-seated resentment which burst forth when provided with the opportunity and a sufficient military vehicle. That these class and political conflicts endured into the post-rebellion period, and indeed produced another attempt at a rising only five years later in 1803, demonstrate that the mentalities which gave rise to them were deeply embedded among the populace and not merely a mindless outburst or *Jaquerie*.

Though the collective action of rebels, yeomen, soldiers and militia ultimately determined the outcome of the uprisings during these years, there was a personal and local dimension to events in Rathcoole that influenced the character of the rising. Political enmities and class antagonisms were acted upon in an often intimate fashion by people who knew one another. In the case of the Clancys, servants turned on their former masters. Meanwhile, betrayals such as that of Ormsby by Rourke, and that of Walsh who informed on his United Irish comrades, also underpinned the personal tenor of events. Local rivalries were played out when 'Crops' and 'Tails' – groups that seemed to blend elements of traditional faction fighting and grander national political rivalries – fought against one another in Ballymount during the maelstrom of a national insurrection.

During the 1790s the United Irishmen brought to the surface the configurations of later movements which would challenge the dominant socio-political order and landed aristocracy. In Rathcoole, local bonds of control began to break down and the upper class, hitherto immune from attack, came to be targeted by those who had silently slaved away in their service for decades. As they had done elsewhere, the United Irishmen transformed Rathcoole, a previously sleepy corner of Co. Dublin, into a hive of political and military activity. And as also occurred in other districts, the rising in Rathcoole was foiled militarily by the use of informants and pre-emptive action by yeomen and the military that forced the rebels into poorly co-ordinated strikes. Had the spy Walsh not liaised with the government, the United Irish forces might have descended from the hills on Rathcoole and held the strategically important village for a number of days. However, nationally, the pendulum swung quickly towards a rebel defeat, faced as they were with a vast spy network and the military might of an empire. Nevertheless, even in defeat, the long-term ramifications of the years 1798–1803 for the locality of Rathcoole, and for the country, were profound. The republican activism, propagandist exploits, and military feats of those years laid the basis for a tradition that has influenced the course of Irish politics and society for well over 200 years.

Notes

ABBREVIATIONS

FJ	*Freeman's Journal*
NAI	National Archives of Ireland
NLI	National Library of Ireland
RP	Rebellion Papers
SPP	State Prisoners' Petitions
TCD	Trinity College Dublin

INTRODUCTION

1 Tommy Graham, 'The transformation of the Dublin Society of United Irishmen into a mass-based revolutionary organisation, 1791–6' in Thomas Bartlett, David Dickson, Dáire Keogh and Kevin Whelan (eds), *1798 – a bicentenary perspective* (Dublin, 2003), pp 136–46.

2 Jim Smyth, *The men of no property: Irish radicals and popular politics in the late eighteenth century* (Dublin, 1992), pp 178–9.

3 Kevin Whelan, 'Politicization in County Wexford and the origins of the 1798 rebellion' in Hugh Gough and David Dickson (eds), *Ireland and the French Revolution* (Dublin, 1990), pp 156–7.

4 James G. Patterson, *In the wake of the great rebellion: republicanism, agrarianism and banditry in Ireland after 1798* (Manchester, 2008), pp 189–90.

5 Raymond Gillespie and Gerard Moran, 'Introduction: writing local history' in Raymond Gillespie and Gerard Moran (eds), *A various country: essays in Mayo history, 1500–1900* (Westport, 1987), pp 18–22.

6 Deirdre Lindsay, 'The rebellion papers', *Journal of the Federation of Ulster Local Studies*, 18:2 (Spring, 1997), 29.

7 The religion of the Clancys has been surmised through tracing their descendant, a 'Mrs Stewart', who is mentioned as having transcribed their correspondence, in the *1911 Census*, to 50 Moat Street, Donaghadee, County Down, where a Church of Ireland family lived.

8 NLI, MS 20,626, *Two notebooks containing transcripts of letters written in 1797–8 by William Clancy and Patrick Clancy of Clondalkin.*

9 Thomas Bartlett, 'Bearing witness: female evidences in courts martial convened to suppress the 1798 rebellion' in Dáire Keogh and Nicholas Furlong (eds), *The women of 1798* (Dublin, 1998), pp 64–8.

10 C.J. Woods, 'R.R. Madden, historian of the United Irishmen' in Bartlett et al. (eds), *1798*, pp 498–9.

11 Patrick Comerford, 'Church of Ireland clergy and the 1798 rising' in Liam Swords (ed.), *Protestant, Catholic and Dissenter: the clergy and 1798* (Dublin, 1997), p. 220.

12 James Kelly, *Sir Richard Musgrave, 1746–1818: ultra-Protestant ideologue* (Dublin, 2009), p. 225.

13 Colm Lennon, *Sixteenth-century Ireland* (2nd ed., Dublin, 2005), pp 302–3.

14 David L. Smith, *A history of the modern British Isles, 1603–1707: the double crown* (Oxford, 1998), pp 45, 176, 296.

15 Gearóid Ó Tuathaigh, *Ireland before the Famine, 1798–1848* (3rd ed., Dublin, 2007), pp 7–11, 37–40.

I. LOCAL SOCIETY AND THE EMERGENCE OF RADICAL POLITICS

1 NLI, MS 16/G/16/50, A map of part of the lands of Rathcool ... laid down by R. Frizell. Mar., 1792.

2 David Broderick, *The first toll-roads: Ireland's turnpike roads, 1729–1858* (Cork, 2002), pp 80, 120.

3 Samuel Lewis, *A topographical dictionary of Ireland* ... 3 vols (London, 1837), ii, p. 492.

4 Richard Griffith, *General valuation of rateable property in Ireland* (Dublin, 1856).

5 Francis Elrington Ball, *A history of the county Dublin ... part third* (Dublin, 1905), p. 124.

6 Thomas Campbell, *A philosophical survey of the south of Ireland* ... (Dublin, 1778), p. 63.

7 Ball, *A history of the county Dublin*, p. 124.

8 *FJ*, 18 Jan. 1791.

9 R.A. Butlin, 'Agriculture in County Dublin in the late eighteenth century', *Studia Hibernica*, 9 (1969), 107.

10 Joseph Archer, *Statistical survey of the county of Dublin* ... (Dublin, 1801), pp 110–11.

11 *Finn's Leinster Journal*, 25 May 1782.

12 *FJ*, 21 Mar. 1793.

13 James Kelly, *Sport in Ireland: 1600–1840* (Dublin, 2014), pp 77, 85–7.

14 John D'Alton, *The history of the county of Dublin* (Dublin, 1838), p. 727.

15 *Census of Ireland, 1861*, pp 42–3.

16 Archer, *Statistical survey of the county of Dublin*, p. 221.

17 Nicholas M. Wolf, *An Irish-speaking island: state, religion, community and the linguistic landscape in Ireland, 1770–1870* (London, 2014), pp 269–70.

18 Caoimhín Ó Cadhla, 'Amhráin Gaeilge 1798' (Dissertation for Graduate Diploma in Irish Folklore, University College Dublin, 2008), pp 27–82.

19 D.H. Akenson, 'Pre-university education, 1782–1870' in W.E. Vaughan (ed.), *A new history of Ireland*; v; *Ireland under the union, i, 1801–1870* (Oxford, 1989), pp 536–7.

20 Michael Quane, 'Mercer's school, Rathcoole and Castleknock, Co. Dublin', *Journal of the Royal Society of Antiquaries of Ireland*, 93:1, pt 1 (1963), 19–21.

21 NLI, Joly Collection, *List of persons who have suffered losses in their property in the city and county of Dublin* ... (Dublin, 1799).

22 Liam Chambers, *Rebellion in Kildare, 1790–1803* (Dublin, 1998), p. 87.

23 *Census of Ireland, 1821*, pp 16–17.

24 *Second report of the commissioners of Irish education inquiry ... 1826*, pp 101–2, H.C. 1826–7 (12), xii, 3.

25 Cormac Ó Gráda, 'School attendance and literacy before the Famine: a simple baronial analysis' in *UCD School for Economic Research: Working Paper Series* (July 2010), pp 1–4.

26 James B. Leslie, *Clergy of Dublin and Glendalough: biographical succession lists* (Belfast, 2001), p. 152.

27 John Gorton, *A topographical dictionary of Great Britain and Ireland*, 3 vols (London, 1833), iii, p. 236.

28 William F.L. Shea, *A short history of Rathcoole: compiled from various sources* (Dublin, 1898), p. 4.

29 Leslie, *Biographical succession lists*, pp 609, 979.

30 Michael Beames, *Peasants and power: the Whiteboy movements and their control in pre-Famine Ireland* (Brighton, 1983), p. 28.

31 'Report on the State of Popery in Ireland, 1731', *Archivium Hibernicum*, 4 (1915), 135.

32 Liam Ó Broin, 'Rathcoole, Co. Dublin, and its neighbourhood: notes on place names, topography and traditions', *Journal of the Royal Society of Antiquaries of Ireland*, 13:3 (1943), 79–97.

33 Ball, *A history of the county Dublin*, p. 124.

34 Archer, *Statistical survey*, p. 202.

35 Seán Bagnall, *Tallaght, 1835–50: a rural place* (Dublin, 2008), p. 59.

36 *Census of Ireland, 1821*, pp 16–17.

37 Ó Tuathaigh, *Ireland before the Famine*, pp 107–9.

38 Butlin, 'Agriculture in County Dublin', 95.

39 D'Alton, *The history of the county of Dublin*, p. 733.

40 NLI, MS 16/G/16/50, A map of part of the lands of Rathcool.

41 Butlin, 'Agriculture in County Dublin', 106.

42 Samuel Lewis, *A history and topography of Dublin city and county* (Dublin, 1980), p. 213.

43 John Sheil O'Grady, 'The history and antiquities of the districts of Rathcoole and Saggart', *Journal of the County Kildare Archaeological Society*, 5 (1908), 75.

44 Kevin Whelan, 'Events and personalities of Newcastle 1600–1850' in Peter O'Sullivan (ed.), *Newcastle Lyons: a parish of the pale* (Dublin, 1986), p. 67.

45 Karina Holton, *Valentine Lawless, Lord Cloncurry, 1773–1853: from United Irishman to liberal politician* (Dublin, 2018), pp 32–8.

46 Whelan, 'Events and personalities of Newcastle 1600–1850', p. 67.

47 W. Porter, *History of the proceedings of the volunteer delegates on the subject of parliamentary reform* (Dublin, 1784), p. 147.

48 *Irish House of Commons Journal, 1783–1785* (4th ed., Dublin, 1797), p. 6.

49 R.R. Madden, *The United Irishmen: their lives and times*, 1st ser., 2nd ed. (Dublin, 1858), p. 589.

50 NAI, SPP, 355.

51 Ball, *A history of the county Dublin*, p. 124.

52 Lewis, *A history and topography of Dublin city and county*, p. 213.

53 *Middlesex Journal or Universal Evening Post*, 10 July 1773.

54 *The Times*, 21 Sept. 1789.

55 Samuel Watson, *The Gentleman and Citizen's Almanack, 1786* (Dublin, 1786), p. 43.

56 W.N. Osborough, 'Arthur Wolfe: first Viscount Kilwarden' in *Oxford dictionary of national biography* (http://www.oxforddnb.com) (accessed 9/8/2016).

57 Ciarán Priestley, *Clonsilla and the rebellion of 1798* (Dublin, 2009), p. 15.

58 NLI, MS 16/G/16/50, *A map of part of the lands of Rathcool*.

59 NAI, SPP, 420.

60 NLI, D. 6941–2, *Lease of lands in Rathcoole by Rev. W. Waller and Sir R. Waller to James Ormsby, 1789*.

61 Whelan, 'Events and personalities of Newcastle 1600–1850', p. 65.

62 *FJ*, 30 June 1785.

63 NAI, SPP, 355.

64 Chambers, *Rebellion in Kildare*, p. 120

65 Thomas Pakenham, *The year of liberty: the great Irish rebellion of 1798* (2nd ed., London, 1997), p. 60.

66 Margaret Ó hÓgartaigh, *Edward Hay, historian of 1798: Catholic politics in an era of*

Wolfe Tone and Daniel O'Connell (Dublin, 2010), pp 20, 45.

67 Ruán O'Donnell, *The rebellion in Wicklow: 1798* (Dublin, 1998), p. 11.

68 R.B. McDowell, 'Proceedings of the Dublin Society of United Irishmen', *Analecta Hibernica*, 17 (1949), 1–7.

69 Graham, 'The transformation' in Bartlett et al., (eds), *1798*, p. 143.

70 Sheil O'Grady, 'The history and antiquities of the districts of Rathcoole and Saggart', 73.

71 R.R. Madden, *The United Irishmen: their lives and times*, 1st ser., 2nd ed., vol. ii (London, 1842), p. 404.

72 Musgrave, *Memoirs of the different rebellions in Ireland ...* (2nd ed., Dublin, 1801), p. 282.

73 Thomas Bartlett, 'An end to the moral economy: the Irish militia disturbances of 1793' in C.H.E. Philpin (ed.), *Nationalism and popular protest in Ireland* (Cambridge, 1987), pp 192–6, 205–6.

74 NLI, PD HP (1779) 4, Francis Wheatley, 'The muster of the Irish volunteers in College Green on the 4th of November, 1779 ...' in *The lady of the house* (Dublin, 1907).

75 Joe Devine, *The house of Corkagh* (Dublin, 2003), pp 7–11.

76 Frank Wright, *Two lands on one soil: Ulster politics before home rule* (New York, 1996), p. 38.

77 Allan Blackstock, 'The Irish yeomanry and the 1798 Rebellion' in Bartlett et al. (eds), *1798*, p. 332.

78 Pádraig Ó Snodaigh, 'Notes on the volunteers, militia, yeomanry and Orangemen of County Wexford', *The Past: the organ of the Uí Cinsealaigh Historical Society*, 14 (1983), 13.

79 *FJ*, 10 Aug. 1781.

80 *FJ*, 7 Oct. 1779.

81 Ó Snodaigh, 'Notes on the volunteers', 13.

82 Blackstock, 'The Irish yeomanry and the 1798 Rebellion', pp 331–44.

83 See the second chapter.

84 Pádraig Ó Snodaigh, 'Volunteers, militia, Orangemen and yeomanry of County Roscommon', *Irish Sword*, 12 (1975–6), 15–35; Ó Snodaigh, 'Notes on the volunteers ... of County Wexford', 5–48.

85   Chambers, *Rebellion in Kildare*, p. 36.
86   Ruán O'Donnell, *Robert Emmet and the rebellion of 1798* (Dublin, 2003), p. 33.
87   Thomas Bartlett, 'Select documents 38: Defenders and Defenderism in 1795', *Irish Historical Studies*, 24:95 (May, 1985), 385.
88   Priestley, *Clonsilla and the rebellion of 1798*, pp 17, 26.
89   *FJ*, 18 Aug. 1795.
90   Chambers, *Rebellion in Kildare*, p. 43.
91   Priestley, *Clonsilla and the rebellion of 1798*, p. 33.
92   Deirdre Lindsay, 'The Fitzwilliam episode revisited' in David Dickson, Dáire Keogh and Kevin Whelan (eds), *The United Irishmen: republicanism, radicalism and rebellion* (Dublin, 1993), pp 204–8.
93   Tommy Graham, '"An union of power?" The United Irish organisation: 1795–1798', in Dickson et al. (eds), *The United Irishmen*, p. 245.
94   Thomas Bartlett, *Ireland: a history* (Cambridge, 2010), pp 217–18.
95   *Eyewitness to 1798*, ed. Terence Folley (Cork, 1996), pp 25–6.
96   David Dickson, 'Taxation and disaffection in late eighteenth-century Ireland' in Samuel Clark and James S. Donnelly Jr. (eds), *Irish peasants: violence and political unrest, 1780–1914* (2nd ed., Manchester, 1986), pp 40–1, 48.
97   Smyth, *The men of no property*, pp 164–9.
98   Daniel Gahan, *The people's rising: Wexford 1798* (Dublin, 1995), p. 3.
99   Graham, 'The United Irish organisation', p. 248.
100 Smyth, *The men of no property*, p. 158.
101 Kevin Whelan, 'The United Irishmen, the enlightenment and popular culture' in Dickson et al. (eds), *The United Irishmen*, p. 279.
102 NLI, MS 20,626, *Two notebooks containing transcripts of letters written in 1797–8 by William Clancy and Patrick Clancy of Clondalkin*, 25 Jan. & 15 Feb. 1798.
103 Kevin Whelan, *The tree of liberty: radicalism, Catholicism and the construction of Irish identity 1760–1830* (Cork, 1996), p. 95.
104 Niall Ó Cíosáin, *Print and popular culture in Ireland, 1750–1850* (2nd ed., Dublin, 2010), pp 216–17.
105 E.P. Thompson, *The making of the English working class* (London, 1963), pp 406–7.
106 *FJ*, 15 July & 1 Dec. 1787.
107 *FJ*, 3 Jan. 1788.
108 *FJ*, 4 Sept. 1784.
109 *The Times*, 18 May 1797.
110 See the second chapter.
111 NLI, *Clancy letters*, 22 Aug. 1797 & 11 Dec. 1798.
112 Ibid., 13 July 1797.
113 Ibid., 5 Jan. 1798.
114 Ibid., 22 Aug. 1797.
115 *FJ*, 16 Sept. 1797.
116 *FJ*, 28 Sept. 1797.
117 *Oracle and Public Advertiser*, 20 Oct. 1797.
118 *FJ*, 13 Oct. 1797.
119 NAI, RP, 620/33/66.
120 NLI, *Clancy letters*, 6 & 25 Jan. 1798.
121 Ibid., 25 Jan. 1798.
122 James Kelly, '"We were all to have been massacred": Irish Protestants and the experience of rebellion' in Bartlett et al., *1798*, p. 317.
123 Madden, *The United Irishmen: their lives and times*, 1st ser., 2nd ed., p. 417.
124 R.R. Madden, *The United Irishmen: their lives and times*, 3rd ser., vol. ii (Dublin, 1846), p. 75.
125 Ibid., p. 84.
126 Blackstock, 'The Irish yeomanry', p. 334.
127 NAI, SPP, 420.
128 Madden, *The United Irishmen: their lives and times*, 3rd ser., vol. ii, p. 76.
129 NAI, SPP, 355.
130 NAI, SPP, 420.
131 Madden, *The United Irishmen: their lives and times*, 3rd ser., vol. ii, p. 76.
132 The 'Lyons of Newcastle' mentioned by the informant is almost certainly Nicholas Lyons who later became highly involved in the rebellion in Kildare alongside Felix Rourke, NAI, RP, 620/51/146.
133 NLI, *Clancy letters*, 12 Mar. 1798.
134 Madden, *The United Irishmen: their lives and times*, 3rd ser., vol. ii, p. 76.
135 NAI, SPP, 355.
136 Musgrave, *Memoirs of the different rebellions*, p. 284.
137 NAI, RP, 620/55/129.
138 *Mirror of the Times*, 24 Mar. 1798.
139 *The Times*, 31 Mar. 1798.
140 NLI, *Clancy letters*, 17 Feb. 1798.
141 Ibid., 17 Feb. 1798.

142 Ibid., 4 Apr. 1798.
143 NAI, RP, 620/37/33.
144 Musgrave, *Memoirs of the different rebellions*, p. 283.

2. THE 1798 REBELLION IN RATHCOOLE

1 Tommy Graham, 'Dublin in 1798: the key to the planned insurrection', in Dáire Keogh and Nicholas Furlong (eds), *The mighty wave: the 1798 rebellion in Wexford* (Dublin, 1996), pp 75–8.
2 Musgrave, *Memoirs of the different rebellions*, p. 280.
3 Ibid., pp 281–2.
4 Both of the Shea brothers escaped transportation for their part in the conspiracy, but the sources do not reveal what became of them afterwards, NAI, SPP, 279, 381.
5 Musgrave, *Memoirs of the different rebellions*, p. 282.
6 NAI, Byrne Papers, M. 5892 a.
7 Musgrave, *Memoirs of the different rebellions*, p. 274.
8 Ibid.
9 NAI, RP, 620/52/156.
10 *The Times*, 31 May 1798.
11 NAI, Byrne Papers, M. 5892 a.
12 Musgrave, *Memoirs of the different rebellions*, p. 274.
13 *London Chronicle*, 26 May 1798.
14 Musgrave, *Memoirs of the different rebellions*, p. 273.
15 *Express and Evening Chronicle*, 26 May 1798.
16 Musgrave, *Memoirs of the different rebellions*, p. 273.
17 *London Chronicle*, 26 May 1798.
18 O'Donnell, *Robert Emmet and the rebellion of 1798*, p. 79.
19 Graham, 'Dublin in 1798', p. 78.
20 Pakenham, *Year of liberty*, p. 135.
21 Madden, *The United Irishmen: their lives and times*, 3rd ser., vol. ii, pp 77, 99.
22 Chambers, *Rebellion in Kildare*, p. 73.
23 Madden, *The United Irishmen: their lives and times*, 3rd ser., vol. ii, pp 77, 99.
24 Chambers, *Rebellion in Kildare*, p. 85.
25 Thomas Bartlett, Kevin Dawson & Dáire Keogh, *Rebellion: an illustrated history* (New York, 1998), p. 116.
26 Musgrave, *Memoirs of the different rebellions*, p. 284.
27 Ibid., p. 282.

28 *Bell's Weekly Messenger*, 10 June 1798.
29 Madden, *The United Irishmen: their lives and times*, 1st ser., vol. ii, p. 404.
30 Stella Tillyard, *Citizen lord: the life of Edward FitzGerald, Irish revolutionary* (New York, 1998), p. 287.
31 Sheil O'Grady, 'The history and antiquities of the districts of Rathcoole and Saggart', p. 74.
32 Ó Broin, 'Rathcoole, Co. Dublin, and its neighbourhood', p. 83.
33 Ibid.
34 Bartlett, *Ireland: a history*, p. 222.
35 *Bell's Weekly Messenger*, 10 June 1798.
36 NAI, SPP, 355.
37 Madden, *The United Irishmen: their lives and times*, 4th series, 2nd ed. (London, 1860), p. 555.
38 Dáire Keogh, '"The most dangerous villain in society": Fr John Martin's mission to the United Irishmen of Wicklow in 1798', *Eighteenth-Century Ireland / Iris an Dá Chultúr*, 7 (1992), 125.
39 NLI, LO 6/1798/35, *An official announcement from the lord lieutenant of the rebel defeats*.
40 Musgrave, *Memoirs of the different rebellions*, p. 371.
41 *St James's Chronicle or the British Evening Post*, 26 June 1798.
42 Musgrave, *Memoirs of the different rebellions*, pp 347–8.
43 Pakenham, *Year of liberty*, p. 126.
44 Musgrave, *Memoirs of the different rebellions*, p. 348.
45 *St James's Chronicle or the British Evening Post*, 26 June 1798.
46 Ó Broin, 'Rathcoole, Co. Dublin, and its neighbourhood', p. 84.
47 *Finn's Leinster Journal*, 7 July 1798.
48 *FJ*, 28 July 1798.
49 NLI, *Clancy letters*, 9 July 1798.
50 Kelly, 'Irish Protestants and the experience of rebellion' in Bartlett et al., *1798*, p. 312.
51 Madden, *The United Irishmen: their lives and times*, 3rd ser., vol. ii, p. 106.
52 Eamon Doyle, *The Wexford insurgents of '98 and their march into Meath* (Enniscorthy, 1997), p. 7.
53 Madden, *The United Irishmen: their lives and times*, 4th ser., 2nd ed., p. 546.
54 Madden, *The United Irishmen: their lives and times*, 3rd ser., vol. ii, p. 78.

55 Doyle, *March into Meath*, p. 10.
56 Madden, *The United Irishmen: their lives and times*, 3rd ser., vol. ii, p. 79.
57 NAI, SPP, 355.
58 Ibid.
59 Doyle, *March into Meath*, p. 18.
60 Madden, *The United Irishmen: their lives and times*, 3rd ser., vol. ii, p. 79.
61 Ibid.
62 NAI, RP, 620/40/46, 620/40/145.
63 NAI, SPP, 355.
64 Madden, *The United Irishmen: their lives and times*, 3rd ser., vol. ii, p. 81.
65 Ibid., p. 83.
66 Cardinal Patrick Francis Moran, *History of the Catholic Church in Australasia: from authentic sources* ... (Sydney, 1895), p. 26.
67 *The Times*, 20 Aug. 1798.
68 *The Observer,* 18 Aug. 1798.
69 *The Times*, 20 Aug. 1798.
70 Madden, *The United Irishmen: their lives and times*, 1st ser., vol. ii, p. 248.
71 Musgrave, *Memoirs of the different rebellions,* p. 282.
72 Madden, *The United Irishmen: their lives and times*, 3rd ser., vol. ii, p. 85.
73 Musgrave, *Memoirs of the different rebellions,* p. 283.
74 TCD, MS 291, Madden Papers.
75 NAI, SPP, 355.
76 NAI, RP, 620/40/46.
77 Madden, *The United Irishmen: their lives and times*, 3rd ser., vol. ii, p. 84.
78 Ibid., pp 77, 85.
79 NAI, RP, 620/40/145.
80 NLI, *Clancy letters*, 16 Sept. 1798.
81 *Mirror of the Times*, 10 Nov. 1798.
82 Musgrave, *Memoirs of the different rebellions,* p. 284.
83 Kevin O'Neill, 'Post-rebellion violence in Ballitore, County Kildare' in Bartlett et al., *1798*, p. 376.
84 NLI, *Clancy letters*, 24 Nov. 1798.
85 NLI, Joly Collection, *List of persons who have suffered losses in their property.*

3. AFTERMATH, 1798–1803

1 Whelan, 'Events and personalities of Newcastle 1600–1850', p. 65.
2 Madden, *The United Irishmen: their lives and times*, 1st ser., 2nd ed., p. 584.
3 NAI, SPP, 355.
4 Ibid.
5 Ruán O'Donnell, *Aftermath: post-rebellion insurgency in Wicklow, 1799–1803* (Dublin, 2000), pp 56–93.
6 NAI, SPP, 355.
7 Madden, *The United Irishmen: their lives and times*, 3rd ser., vol. ii, p. 88.
8 Chambers, *Rebellion in Kildare*, p. 104.
9 Patterson, *In the wake of the great rebellion,* p. 188.
10 *The Times*, 23 Jan. 1799.
11 Ibid., 28 Feb. 1799.
12 *FJ,* 5 Mar. 1799.
13 'Petition of Rev. James Harold, 1799', *Reportorium Novum: Dublin Diocesan Historical Record*, 1:2 (1956), 499.
14 Madden, *The United Irishmen: their lives and times*, 3rd ser., vol. ii, p. 88.
15 A.M. Whitaker, *Unfinished revolution: United Irishmen in New South Wales, 1800–1810* (Sydney, 1994), p. 50.
16 Harold Perkins, 'Harold, James (1744–1830)' in *Australian dictionary of biography*, 1 (Melbourne, 1966), pp 512–13.
17 NAI, SPP, 355.
18 Madden, *The United Irishmen: their lives and times*, 3rd ser., vol. ii, p. 93.
19 Ibid., p. 87.
20 Ibid.
21 NLI, *Clancy letters*, 31 Oct. 1798.
22 Ibid., 11 Dec. 1798.
23 D. George Boyce, *Nineteenth-century Ireland: the search for stability* (2nd ed., Dublin, 2005), p. 23.
24 *Albion and Evening Advertiser*, 17 June 1800.
25 *FJ,* 5 Feb. 1801.
26 NLI, D 10,411, *Mortgage of James Ormsby to David Latouche 1801.*
27 Chambers, *Rebellion in Kildare*, p. 109.
28 Ibid.
29 Lewis, *A history and topography of Dublin city and county*, p. 207.
30 NAI, SPP, 355.
31 NAI, RP, 620/57/111/1.
32 NAI, RP, 620/57/111/2.
33 T.B. Howell, *A complete collection of state trials, xxviii* (London, 1820), p. 959.
34 Madden, *The United Irishmen: their lives and times*, 3rd ser., vol. ii, p. 94.
35 Patrick M. Geoghegan, *Robert Emmet: a life* (Dublin, 2002), pp 116–22.
36 Madden, *The United Irishmen: their lives and times*, 3rd ser., vol. ii, p. 94.

37 O'Donnell, *Robert Emmet and the rising of 1803*, p. 57.
38 R.R. Madden, *The United Irishmen: their lives and times*, 3rd ser., vol. iii (Dublin, 1846), p. 120.
39 Ibid.
40 O'Donnell, *Robert Emmet and the rising of 1803*, pp 87–93.
41 Madden, *The United Irishmen: their lives and times*, 3rd ser., vol. ii, p. 94.
42 NAI, RP, 620/64/179.
43 NAI, Byrne Papers, M. 5892 a.
44 O'Donnell, *Robert Emmet and the rising of 1803*, p. 91.
45 *FJ*, 9 Aug. 1803.
46 O'Donnell, *Robert Emmet and the rising of 1803*, p. 92.
47 *FJ*, 28 July 1803, Booth had probably been motivated, at least in part, to join the yeomanry as a consequence of having his family home plundered earlier in 1787, *FJ*, 1 Dec. 1787.
48 *The Scots magazine; or, general repository of literature, history ... vol. 65* (Edinburgh, 1803), p. 573.
49 Madden, *The United Irishmen: their lives and times*, 3rd ser., vol. ii, p. 95.
50 Howell, *State trials, xxviii*, pp 930, 935–6.
51 Ibid., p. 947.
52 Ibid., pp 952, 971.
53 Madden, *The United Irishmen: their lives and times*, 3rd ser., vol. ii, p. 95.
54 Howell, *State trials, xxviii*, p. 992.
55 *FJ*, 13 Sept. 1803.
56 Madden, *The United Irishmen: their lives and times*, 3rd ser., vol. ii, p. 96.
57 *The Times*, 25 Feb. 1804.
58 *Johnson's British Gazette and Sunday Monitor*, 18 Sept. 1803.
59 Madden, *The United Irishmen: their lives and times*, 3rd ser., vol. ii, p. 96.
60 Maeve Mulryan Moloney, *A history of Saggart and Rathcoole parishes* (Walkinstown, 1998), p. 97.
61 Howell, *State trials, xxviii*, p. 1052.
62 Madden, *The United Irishmen: their lives and times*, 3rd ser., vol. ii, p. 114.
63 Madden, *The United Irishmen: their lives and times*, 3rd ser., vol. iii, p. 106.
64 *Papers presented to the House of Commons, respecting state prisoners confined in Kilmainham Gaol, Dublin, 1804*, p. 471, H.C. 1805 (90) vi, 39–40.
65 TCD, Madden Papers, 329.
66 Madden, *The United Irishmen: their lives and times*, 3rd ser., vol. iii, p. 106.

CONCLUSION

1 Kelly, 'Irish Protestants and the experience of rebellion' in Bartlett et al. (eds), *1798*, p. 330.